Exploring the Little-Known New Testament

Everyday Stories

Exploring the Little-Known New Testament

Everyday Stories

LUCAS PARK BOOKS

ST. LOUIS, MISSOURI

Published by Lucas Park Books

Scripture quotations, unless otherwise indicated, are identified and taken from the following:

All other sources are listed and credited in Appendix 2: Notes.

Italics, **Bold**, and ALL CAPS used in quotations reflect the author's added emphasis.

ISBN: 9781603500401

Printed in the United States of America

Table of Contents

Introduction and Welcome   vii

Philemon   1

   1. Risky Generosity (1-11)
   2. Freedom Running (12-25)

James   9

   3. Troubled Opportunities (1:1-4)
   4. Surf's Up! (1 5-8)
   5. The Big Fade (1:9-12)
   6. Spirit-Showers (1:13-18)
   7. In One Ear and... (1:19-27)
   8. Abnormal Invitations (2:1-13)
   9. Seamless Faith (2:14-26)
  10. Open Mouth, Insert.... (3:1-12)
  11. Wisdom Seeds (3:13-18)
  12. Which Side? (4:1-10)
  13. Haven't You Heard? (4:11-17)
  14. Who's Gonna Know? (5:1-6)
  15. Final Instructions (5:7-20)

First Peter   53

  16. On Assignment (1:1-7)
  17. Tug of...Grace (1:8-16)
  18. Ring in the New...Life! (1:17-25)
  19. Trash to Treasure (2:1-10)
  20. Temporary Quarters (2:11-17)
  21. Silent Grace (2:18-25)
  22. Holy Advantage (3:1-7)
  23. Blessed Blessing (3:8-14)
  24. Mud Bath! (3:15-22)
  25. Quick Thinking! (4:1-11)
  26. A Refinery...Here? (4:12-19)
  27. Real Jesus - Real Church (5:1-14)

Second Peter   95

28. Grace Leak! (1:1-9)
29. Key Witness (1:10-15)
30. Light-Weight (1:16-21)
31. Downhill Slide (2:1-9)
32. Return to Sender (2:10-22)
33. Loss Prevention (3:1-13)
34. Twist and Spin (3:14-18)

First John   119

35. Light-Soaked (chapter 1)
36. In…or Out? (2:1-6)
37. Up Close and Personal (2:7-14)
38. Deep Connections (2:15-25)
39. Holy Childhood (2:26 - 3:3)
40. Love…Who? (3:4-10)
41. Love Practice Time! (3:11-24)
42. Origin-al Evidence (4:1-6)
43. The Love Virus (4:7-12)
44. Love-Standing (4:13-21)
45. Who Wins? (5:1-12)
46. Fax Faith? (5:13-21)

Second John   155

47. Due Diligence (1-6)
48. Intruder Alert! (7-18)

Third John   161

49. Strange Hospitality (1-8)
50. Model-Building (9-15)

Jude   167

51. Behind Holy Lines (1-7)
52. Lost in Time and Space (8-16)
53. Centered Life (17-25)

Appendix #1 – Bible Translations and How to Find Them   177

Appendix #2 – Notes   179

About the author   180

Introduction and Welcome!

Bible. Study. These are two words which many (maybe even you) have not been too enthusiastic about. For many, the word 'Bible' is connected with rules and restrictions. Not just that, but what could it possibly have to do with life today? Written thousands of years ago, hasn't it lost its relevance? In a word, no.

And what about the word 'study'? Now there's an exciting word (not)! Let's see, how about the image of long boring hours spent learning things you'll never need? Didn't you leave all that behind when you got out of school?

I want you to try on some new words: experience, explore, and everyday. Let's call them the 'three e's'. What would it be like to experience the Bible texts in your life, right here and now? How about exploring the stories in the setting of your everyday world?

The Exploring...Everyday Stories Bible experience series seeks to help you do just that. You may be someone who has never read the Bible. Maybe you don't even own one! Perhaps you've been in and out of churches all your life, but you've never really connected 'The Book' to your real everyday life. If so, then welcome to the Bible in 'three e's'!

This series is designed to be experienced individually or in groups who are sharing the exploration together. All the Scripture passages are printed in this book, so if you don't own a Bible or yours is hard for you to understand, wait a bit before you purchase one.

You will experience four Bible translations/versions in this exploration journey: (1) The New Revised Standard Version; (2) The New Living Translation; (3) The Contemporary English Version; and (4) The Message Version. Each is described in Appendix 1 of this book along with a purchasing source should you decide to buy one or more of them.

In each chapter, you will read a section of Scripture. Most times, it will be presented in two or more translations/versions, so you can experience the 'flavor' of each. Then you will read an 'everyday' story related to the Scripture, followed by a connection between the Bible passage and the story. Finally, reflection questions are presented to guide you in further thought and exploration.

Like many of you, I came to a place in my own life where I wondered about the relevance of the Bible to my real, everyday life. Then my eyes were opened as God led me to connect things going on today in everyday life with Bible texts. It is my hope and prayer that this exploration experience will lead you to new excitement and growth in your spiritual life. May God richly bless your explorations, may you experience the Holy Spirit in new and powerful ways, and may your eyes be opened to the real presence of Christ in your everyday life!

Rev. Dr. Al W. Adams

Philemon

■

1

■

Risky Generosity

This letter is from Paul, in prison for preaching the Good News about Christ Jesus, and from our brother Timothy. It is **written to Philemon,** our much loved co-worker, and to our sister Apphia and to Archippus, a fellow soldier of the cross. **I am also writing to the church that meets in your house.** May God our Father and the Lord Jesus Christ give you grace and peace.

I always thank God when I pray for you, Philemon, because **I keep hearing of your trust in the Lord Jesus and your love for all of God's people. You are generous because of your faith.** And I am **praying that you will really put your generosity to work, for in so doing you will come to an understanding of all the good things we can do for Christ.**

I myself have gained much joy and comfort from your love, my brother, because your kindness has so often refreshed the hearts of God's people. That is why I am boldly asking a favor of you. **I could demand it in the name of Christ because it is the right thing for you to do,** but because of our love, I prefer just to ask you. So take this as a request from your friend Paul, an old man, now in prison for the sake of Christ Jesus.

My plea is that you show kindness to Onesimus. I think of him as my own son because he became a believer as a result of my ministry here in prison. Onesimus hasn't been of much use to you in the past, but now he is very useful to both of us.

- Philemon 1-11 (New Living Translation)

* * * * * * * * *

"You know, **I've had it easy so far.** Went to church all my life, taught my kids about Jesus, tried to always show them how we should behave like Christians. My son told me just the other day how much he respects me for the way I raised him. He said having kids of his own, well, it made him realize it wasn't always easy. But now, well, **now THIS is different."**

Irv lowered his gaze from mine and shook his head. As I continued to listen, he opened my eyes to something I'd never thought of. "Yep, **who'd have ever thought moving to this place would give me one more chance to teach my kids about being a real, living Christian?"**

I could tell Irv was on a roll – and I was waiting to hear more. He didn't disappoint me.
"See that nurse down the hall there? Mike's his name. Well, **when he found out I was 'one of those Christians',** **he quit being sociable.** Not one good conversation since then. And **Mabel – she's my neighbor – she's just**

plain mean! I think 'Hmph!' is the only word she still remembers – either that or somebody changed my name without telling me!" He winked a mischief-sparkled eye at me.

"You **know what Bill – that's my son – reminded me about yesterday?** He was telling me about how **his son – that'd be my grandson Walter – had this bully-kid sitting next to him in class.** Then Bill said the most remarkable thing! He said that Mabel next door could be the spitting image of this bully kid, all grown up. Apparently all this classroom neighbor of Walter's does is – are you ready? – says 'Hmph!' as she knocks stuff of his desk and tries to trip him. **Guess what Bill told the boy?"**

I couldn't resist hearing about this, and "What?" popped out of my mouth before I knew it. I was hooked – I just had to know!

"Well, **my Bill told Walter he just had to be just like grandpa! He just had to act like he knew Jesus.** Can you believe it? Like me! Well, that got me to thinking about Mabel here and nurse Mike. It was just like God reached down and grabbed my spirit. And do you know what Bill said next? He looked right at me, just like I taught him to do when he was serious, and he told me he'd passed on just what I'd always told him. 'Remember what you used to tell us kids, Pop?', he said, **'You said 'Generosity is risky. Look what it cost God.' And then you'd always hug me and say, 'Our God is a generous God Who risked it all for us. Now let's act like we know it!'"**

His eyes twinkled again. "Bet you're wondering where I'm going with all this, don't you? Well, I've **decided to follow my own teaching, well, more like God's teaching** anyway. I'm just going to remember how much God misses having a relationship with Mabel and Mike. I'm going to pray for them. Why just this morning I told them both I was praying for them, and you know what they said to that? Well, I'll tell you. Mabel, well, I bet you can guess – she said her usual (but louder) 'Hmph', but you know what? She turned around and looked at me – really looked at me – for the first time in the four months I've lived here. And nurse Mike, well, he just gave me a weird look, but I know he heard me, and soon I hope he hears God too. **I know without a doubt that God can use them in mighty ways!"**

So how about it? Paul challenged Philemon to look at Onesimus and realize that God's risky generosity extended even to this man who had been Philemon's slave. Philemon was to recognize in Onesimus a brother in Christ.

But wait! Slavery was a reality in society then – what would the neighbors say? This generosity that Paul asks of Philemon was truly risky. Why, what would other slaves in the neighborhood think? No matter, Paul still challenged Philemon to live his faith.

God challenges us in much the same way. Our God of eternally risky generosity calls us to tune our lives to follow Christ's example.

Who is the 'Onesimus' in your life right now? Maybe, like many of us, you have even more than one! Irv discovered his in his neighbor Mabel and nurse Mike.

You see, **Jesus' instruction to 'Go and make disciples' (Matthew 28: 19) begins with just this: risky generosity!**

Reflections

Think about your life. How could you be identified as a follower of Christ?

What if you were a neighbor of Philemon? A friend and fellow-slave of Onesimus?

How is God challenging you in similar ways?

2

Freedom Running

Onesimus hasn't been of much use to you in the past, but now he is very useful to both of us. I am sending him back to you, and with him comes my own heart. I really wanted to keep him here with me while I am in these chains for preaching the Good News, and he would have helped me on your behalf.

But I didn't want to do anything without your consent. And **I didn't want you to help because you were forced to do it but because you wanted to.**

Perhaps you could think of it this way: Onesimus ran away for a little while so you could have him back forever. He is no longer just a slave; he is a beloved brother, especially to me. Now he will mean much more to you, both as a slave and as a brother in the Lord.

So if you consider me your partner, give him the same welcome you would give me if I were coming. If he has harmed you in any way or stolen anything from you, charge me for it. I, Paul, write this in my own handwriting: "I will repay it." **And I won't mention that you owe me your very soul!**

Yes, dear brother, please do me this favor for the Lord's sake. Give me this encouragement in Christ. I am confident as I write this letter that you will do what I ask and even more!

Please keep a guest room ready for me, for I am hoping that God will answer your prayers and let me return to you soon. Epaphras, my fellow prisoner in Christ Jesus, sends you his greetings. So do Mark, Aristarchus, Demas, and Luke, my co-workers. **The grace of the Lord Jesus Christ be with your spirit.**

- Philemon 11-25 (New Living Translation)

* * * * * * * * *

"You know that kid who came to see you yesterday?", the voice asked as soon as Mike picked up his office phone. Sitting in his small office in the back of the guys' locker room, he wished the old rickety air conditioner would kick in soon to get the ninety-plus degree temperature down. At least maybe it would blow some air his way. He ran a workout towel across his forehead as he tried to clear his mind and focus on the mystery caller. *I know this voice...who IS it?*

A first year varsity track coach, Mike felt like he was running a constant sprint in this week before school started. Lately his life had been a whirlwind of meetings, tryouts, calls from colleges, and scheduling nightmares, not to mention what felt like a million messages from parents.

"Mike, you there buddy?" ***Wow, a voice from the past!*** *What could Mitch, his old college coach, want?*

"Hey Mitch. Can I call you back? I mean, I'm a bit crazy right now. Or I could call you tonight…."
"Nope, this can't wait. **Remember a kid who came to ask you about track yesterday?** Kind of tall, skinny, blond hair…..?"

Mike tried to remember a tall blond kid. **Realization hit him like a cold, wet blanket.** "You mean the one who couldn't even talk? That one?" *What on earth could Coach have to do with THAT kid?* Mitch's voice cut through his thoughts. **"Did you let him try out?"** *Coach Mitch couldn't be serious, right?*

"You serious, Coach? I mean, he couldn't even talk!" Mike began shuffling papers, trying to brinh some order to the chaos on his desk.

Mitch kept at him. "He bring you a note? Little green piece of paper, folded in half?"
Oh yeah - THAT note. "Let me look around here….oh yeah, here it is." Mike spotted the corner of the paper sticking out from a paper stack. Realizing it was a note from Mitch, he quickly read it.
 "Hey Mike, this kid's name is Jess. Let him run, OK? Then call me tomorrow and tell me what you think. Coach Mitch"

"Mike? Hey, Mike, you there? **You didn't let him run, did you?"**
Silence soaked the air as sweat ran down Mike's face. He scrambled for his next words. Mitch knew him so well. He'd been there for Mike through so much. *How could he let his old coach down?*

Coach Mitch took advantage of the silence. "You know, **Jess has run in the Special Olympics since he was six years old, but they quit letting him run a couple of years ago.** Anything he ran, he won. I don't mean barely, either. He won by almost ridiculous margins. Finally they told him he needed to get on a 'regular' team, so I've been working with him. **He may be deaf, and he may not talk so well,** but this kid can run for sure. He's in a spot, kind of like another long-shot kid I knew some years back. Right, Mike?"

Mike was catching on now. **Coach was on a personal mission for this kid.** "Ah, OK Coach, I get it. Do the kid a favor. Well, it couldn't hurt. After all, you sure helped me; the least I can do is try the kid. OK. I'll see what I can do."

He hung up the phone, still thinking. Reaching for the workout towel again to swab the sweat on his face, **Mike let memories flood his head.** He remembered his own first 'Coach talk' with Mitch. The cops had caught him and some of his old friends **snorting cocaine under the bleachers** after the football game, and **Coach Mitch had come to the juvie lockup to visit.**

"Hey bud," Coach had begun, as the shock of a teacher caring enough to come all the way downtown to see him began to wear off, **"Saw you running from the cops last night. Ever think of running track?** You were really fast out there." Mitch paused, reading the look on young Mike's face. Mike remembered thinking, *wow, this guy's crazy. I'm sure he wants to run a druggie like me on the track team. Druggie Jock. Yeah, right, sure.* But that had been the deal. Make every practice, work hard, and keep regular 'chat' appointments with the Coach, and they'd let him out. **Little did he know then how much Coach Mitch would change his life.**

Coach Mitch had literally freed Mike from slavery - to drugs and a downhill life. Very few (if any) people would connect the scrawny coke-addicted teenager of back then to the strong healthy coach with the clear gaze and easy style of today.

So Mike decided to give Jess a try. He picked up the phone and called Coach Mitch back. "Can you have Jess at practice tomorrow? It's the last one before our first big meet. I'll see what he's got, OK?" Mitch's answer was fast. "Yep, we'll be there. See ya."

Jess was phenomenal. He was so fast the team just stared as he ran mock races in practice. He took both the 60 and the mile in the next meet...by a long shot. Coach Mitch's sideline grin was so big, Mike thought for sure his teeth would fall out. Yep, Coach had brought Mike a real treasure in young Jess. Soon he was known as the "long shot kid" around the track locker room.

* * * * * * * * * *

How does God take a 'long shot' on us? I mean, when you consider humanity's 'track record', the chances don't seem so promising, do they?

But that's exactly what God does. **Just like Paul freeing Onesimus from slavery,** God sent Jesus to free us forever from slavery to sin. **Just like Paul sent Onesimus back** a changed and freed man, God frees us in Christ and sends us back into the world as parts of the Body of Christ - the church - to spread the Good News so others may be freed and given new life as well.

With the eternal (and incredible) Gift that is Jesus the Christ, **God says to us, "I will (and have) repay (repaid) it." Are we living as freed slaves?** Are we seeking to show the way to freedom for others? There's always room on God's 'track team'. Who are we inviting to join us? As Paul says to Philemon, "...give him the same welcome you would give me if I were coming."

Let's welcome someone this week to church - God's 'team practice'!

Reflections

Have you ever been given a chance when you had given up hope? If so, how did that feel?

Have you ever given someone a chance who thought they were out of chances? How was that for you?

How are Christians "freed slaves"? Does that affect how you live and see the world?

Reflections (continued)

What is there about people who truly live as freed followers of Christ that attracts others?

Which character do you identify with most in this story? Why?

James

3

Troubled Opportunities

This letter is from James, a slave of God and of the Lord Jesus Christ. It is written to Jewish Christians scattered among the nations. Greetings!

*Dear brothers and sisters, **whenever trouble comes your way, let it be an opportunity for joy.*** For when your faith is tested, your endurance has a chance to grow. So let it grow, for when your endurance is fully developed, ***you will be strong in character and ready for anything.***

- James 1: 1-4 (New Living Translation)

I, James, am a slave of God and the Master Jesus, writing to the twelve tribes scattered to Kingdom Come: Hello!

Consider it a sheer gift, friends, when tests and challenges come at you from all sides. You know that ***under pressure, your faith-life is forced into the open and shows its true colors.*** So don't try to get out of anything prematurely. ***Let it do its work so you become mature and well-developed,*** *not deficient in any way.*

- James 1: 1-4 (The Message Version)

* * * * * * * * * *

One mile. It seemed impossible. Yet that was the requirement to be a certified lifeguard. Adam spent two hours every morning swimming before heading to work. The certification test would begin in five minutes, and his mind swirled. **Could he do it?**

Adam stripped off his sweats and shoved them into his locker. **Memories of his failed attempt** to make the mile last time began to creep into the edges of his mind. He remembered that feeling of going under, his last bit of strength gone, and it threatened to infiltrate and destroy his mental preparation for today's attempt. It had been just last week in this very pool that he'd come up short of that mile - by just two laps.

He made his way poolside and took his position, selecting the outside lane. Adam figured at least if he started to go down like last week, he'd be closer to help. Back then, he'd been out in the **middle of the pool where he'd almost drowned** trying to get under all the lane-marking ropes to the safety of the pool's edge.

The **starting signal sounded**, and Adam began swimming. This time, he remembered what his instructor taught him about pacing. He hit a steady pace this time from the start. Time seemed to fly as he made five laps, then ten, then twenty. He **began to pray in rhythm with his strokes.**

Almost there. Almost. *Man, just like last week.* Again, the thoughts of failure threatened to sap his strength and concentration. *No! Not like last week!* Amazingly the response in his mind seemed to come automatically, and he felt a new strength as he resumed his praying and swimming, soon hitting a rhythm once more.

One more lap. Adam could see the finish. Closer and closer. *Thank you God, Thank you God*, he thought over and over as his hands pulled the water back over and over.

"Thank you, God!" erupted from his throat as his hand hit the pool wall at the end of his mile swim. The official looked down at him, a surprised look on her face. "I've heard lots of things yelled when people made it, but that's a first. I like it!" She smiled at Adam as he recovered in the shallow end of the pool. "Congratulations. You made it!"

Adam hoisted himself up to sit on the edge of the pool where he'd left his prosthetic leg. It wasn't until he stood that many of the observers who'd gathered for the next event noticed. Wounded in Afghanistan, Adam had just one leg. Used to people's surprised reactions, he laughed as his accomplishment finally sunk in. "Bet **I'll be the only one-legged lifeguard** in L.A. - but I hope not for long! You see, I've got two buddies who thought I was crazy. Deal was, if I made it today, they're next."

As he stepped into the recreation center parking lot, **Adam didn't expect the cameras** and reporters. They closed in as they realized who he was. **"What do you have to say?"**, they asked. He thought for a minute. "I say stick with it. Whatever you're trying to accomplish, **don't let temporary failure stop you. Let it teach you, grow you up."** He paused. "And thank God. I know lots of people say it when they win, but **thank God for those failures too.** Thank God for using them to bring you closer to the strength you need, for bringing you through the tough times when you think you'll never get there. I guess that's it." And with that, he climbed in his car and headed for work.

$$* \quad * \quad * \quad * \quad * \quad * \quad * \quad * \quad *$$

Without trials (and failures too), we just wouldn't learn much. It's a truth that most of us don't like to hear. It's what we do in the tough times that determines where we'll go next. Do we wallow, you know, the 'poor me' attitude? Many times we do, at least for a while. But then what?

Adam had been trying (and failing) to make that mile qualifying swim for six months before he made it that day. Many people had told him how crazy he was, a one-legged guy trying to swim a mile! **He almost gave up.** Almost. Then a friend and Army buddy challenged him to think and pray about where God was leading him through all this failure and frustration. When he began to change his focus from himself to God, Adam found he could swim longer each time he tried. Finally he made it - one mile - and earned his lifeguard certificate.

Then came the next hard part. Who'd hire a one-legged lifeguard? Most wouldn't. But as it turned out, the local marina swimming spot was owned by a veteran who decided to give Adam a chance. Good choice. Three weeks later, television news video showed him saving a little girl who'd been pulled out into the deep water by the current.

That's the deal, you see. We're called to use the God-strength we gain through our struggles to, as many say, 'fail forward'. **James is telling us to use our troubles** - our struggles and failures - as opportunities to gain strength and maturity. **Let God into your struggles and failures.** Allow God to transform your troubled times into troubled...<u>opportunities</u>. Allow grace to mature you, strengthen you, and bring you incredible spiritual growth!

Reflections

How does God use our hard times to strengthen us? Has God done this in your life? How?

How does making it through our tough times enable us to be helpful to others as they face similar challenges? What examples can you think of from your own life or that of someone you know?

How can a church community stand with and support people who are experiencing struggles and hard times? Think of these kinds of challenges: financial; emotional; spiritual; physical.

4

Surf's Up!

If you need wisdom-- if you want to know what God wants you to do-- ask him, and he will gladly tell you. He will not resent your asking. **But when you ask him, be sure that you really expect him to answer, for a doubtful mind is as unsettled as a wave of the sea that is driven and tossed by the wind.** *People like that should not expect to receive anything from the Lord. They can't make up their minds. They waver back and forth in everything they do.*
– James 1: 5-8 (New Living Translation)

If any of you is lacking in wisdom, ask God, who gives to all generously and ungrudgingly, and it will be given you. But **ask in faith, never doubting, for the one who doubts is like a wave of the sea, driven and tossed by the wind;** *for the doubter, being double-minded and unstable in every way, must not expect to receive anything from the Lord.*
– James 1: 5-8 (New Revised Standard Version)

* * * * * * * * *

Vacation - finally! In that place between being asleep and awake, Brad felt the cool ocean breeze wash across the bed. *Ahhh...* Light crept into his hotel room as excited voices filtered through the balcony screen doors.

"Surf's up!" He heard the excited voice followed quickly by the sound of slamming doors, running feet, and a few loud shouts of "Whoo-hoo!".

This was Brad's dream vacation of a lifetime - two weeks of beach, sun, and surfing - courtesy of his Uncle Aaron. Two weeks to learn how to surf, perfect his tan, and get that perfect 'surfer dude' look he wanted to take to college next month.

Brad jumped out of bed, yanked his shorts on, and headed for the bathroom. He looked back briefly as the **"Surfing 4 Dummies" book he'd bought at the airport crashed to the floor.** Three minutes later, he was locking his hotel room door and heading for the beach.

"Surfing Lessons Here!" Brad saw the sign and headed straight for the little beach shack with the neat rows of surf boards lined up outside. *Great!* As he hurried across the sand, he fished the 'free lesson' coupon out of his pocket.

"Hey, I heard the surf's up!", Brad began as he got the attention of the guy sitting on the porch waxing a surf board. The hand rubbing wax into the board stopped - for a second. Looking up into Brad's excited, expectant face, he smiled - and returned to his waxing.

"Been surfing before?" At Brad's blank look, he shook his head - and kept waxing. "Name's Mike. **'Round here, we read the surf before we ride it. Read....THEN ride.** That's the rule. Know how to read?"

Oh boy. **Disappointment threatened** to ruin the day's great start. Mike looked up at Brad again. He'd seen the look on these vacationers - a lot. "Hey, you seem like a smart guy. Bet you did some listening and learning before you got behind the wheel to drive, right?"

Where was THIS going? Brad was really wondering about this guy now. *Maybe if I humor him, he'll rent me a board, and I can get surfing....*

"OK, here's how it is. You take this board. You see a wave. You jump in. You swim out. You try to ride it. You drown - or worse - see those rocks down the beach? You meet them, up close and personal. So, Brad, is it? Well, Brad, **smart guys read, THEN ride. Want some reading lessons?"**

✸ ✸ ✸ ✸ ✸ ✸ ✸ ✸ ✸ ✸

"If you need wisdom-- **if you want to know what God wants you to do-- ask him, and he will gladly tell you."** **Ask. Listen. THEN act.** It's the spiritual equal to Mike the surfing instructor's rule of "read, THEN ride". So many times in life we act, then wonder where God is! **Like Brad, we're so ready to get going that we don't stop to look where we're headed!**

This Scripture tells us, But when you ask him, be sure that you really expect him to answer, for **a doubtful mind is as unsettled as a wave of the sea that is driven and tossed by the wind."** Soon we too may find ourselves either drowning or on the rocks. Mike's warning is echoed in this Scripture. Surfers learn to watch and 'read' the waves and currents before they decide what to do. Many times we decide what we're going to do, THEN we ask God to go along and make it happen. Scripture tells us we've got it backwards - we too should read, THEN ride - ask and listen to God, THEN act!

Each day when we get up, **life calls out "Surf's Up!"** to us in many different ways. Will we simply jump in (remember drowning and big rocks)? Or will we take time to be with God first, in prayer-conversation, asking and listening for guidance?

If we'll just take the time to be truly attentive to our God-relationship, God will indeed give, as this Scripture says, *"generously and ungrudgingly"* to us. In God's Presence and with His guidance, we will truly 'surf' through life surrounded by God's grace and power!

Reflections

In what ways is the "surf up" in your life right now?

What and/or who do you look to for guidance?

How do you deal with those times when you are tempted, like Mike, to "surf, then read"?

5

The Big Fade

Let the believer who is lowly boast in being raised up, and the rich in being brought low, because the rich will disappear like a flower in the field. For the sun rises with its scorching heat and withers the field; its flower falls, and its beauty perishes. It is the same way with the rich; in the midst of a busy life, they will wither away.

Blessed is anyone who endures temptation. Such a one has stood the test and will receive the crown of life that the Lord has promised to those who love him.

– James 1: 9-12 (New Revised Standard Version)

When down-and-outers get a break, cheer! And when the arrogant rich are brought down to size, cheer! Prosperity is as short-lived as a wildflower, so don't ever count on it. You know that as soon as the sun rises, pouring down its scorching heat, the flower withers. Its petals wilt, and, before you know it, that beautiful face is a barren stem. Well, that's a picture of the "prosperous life". At the very moment everyone is looking on in admiration, it fades away to nothing.

Anyone who meets a testing challenge head-on and manages to stick it out is mighty fortunate. For such persons loyally in love with God, the reward is life and more life.

- James 1: 9-12 (The Message Version)

* * * * * * * * * *

"You know, I've spent my whole life working in the theater, helping young people discover the joy of acting, of telling a story well. **Lately, as I lay here in this bed, I'm just waiting for that final curtain, that final act.** I just want to know, will it be like some of my friends say, just a big 'fade to black' - with nothing on the other side? Or will it be like my Christian friends tell me: the biggest 'fade to Light' I could ever imagine?

Craig was young to be facing this question. **At thirty-seven young years of age,** his back had begun hurting badly just a few weeks before. Now diagnosed with colon cancer, they'd told him just that morning he had only weeks left to live. **So what would it be like?**

As we sat in his room and thought back over his many theater stories, Craig realized he had indeed faced tough challenges and 'stuck it out', as the Scripture says. So what would the reward, this 'more life' look like?

"You know, lots of times lately, **when the pain gets really bad, that 'fade to black' sounds mighty good. I just don't want to feel anything any more.** I just want this to be over. Did I tell you about Mick, the rich old guy who helped us get started with the theater company?" I nodded a 'no', and Craig smiled. I could tell these were happy memories for him. As he pressed the button for more morphine, he told me Mick's story.

"Well, **this rich guy came to one of our first 'in the park' shows** - 'Wizard of Oz', it was. Anyway, he showed up. Fancy car, nice suit, the works. I remember thinking, *Boy, he's really slumming coming around here! Maybe he's lost or something....* So he started talking, just talking - to the set crew, the stage guys, you name it. **He stayed for the show. It rained. He still stayed.** By the second act, we'd shut down the electronics - you know, open air show, rain....not good. So here we were in the drizzle, costumes getting droopier and droopier. Thing was, we couldn't afford to give refunds, so as they say, the show went on. This Mick guy came up to me after the show. **'Would you like to have a real place - inside** - to do these shows? Your company's good. Really good. How about it?' I know he saw my disbelief. **Where did he think we'd get the money for that?** Know what he said next? He told me, 'Can't take it with me when I die, can I? Might as well help some folks do good work, right? Here's the address, and my card. Call me tomorrow and we'll get you set up. Deal?' And that was the beginning."

I asked Craig if he thought Mick was living a 'fade to black' or a 'fade to Light' kind of life. He thought for a few minutes. "Fade to Light" was his answer. "Yep, Mick knew there was more to life than this." He waved his hand around the room. "Now that you mention it, they thought they'd lost me the other night. I don't know what happened. Interesting though, when I came to, they said just that - 'We thought we'd lost you' - but I felt less lost than I've ever felt in my life. Go figure! You know, I think I've answered my own question. Definitely 'fade to Light'. Definitely."

I heard a few weeks later that Craig died just a week or so after our visit. Someone **showed me a copy of his funeral program.** Under a wonderful picture of Craig (dressed as the lion from Wizard of Oz) was this title: "Fade to.......LIGHT!!"

* * * * * * * * * *

So how about your life? Are you living a 'fade to black' life? You know, the kind of life some people call 'get it all while you can'? Or are your sights set a bit higher, a bit farther ahead - to the eternal? In other words, are you living a 'fade to Light' life like Craig's friend Mick?

Either way, Mick's right when he said **you can't take it with you.** So do we try to do it all, get it all, now, before it's 'too late'? What's too late anyway?

Remember, **true life is more than we can see now,** more than we can even imagine now. True life is God's 'crown of life' God's 'life and more life'. Life in this world tempts us, luring us constantly to focus on what we can get, what we can experience here and now. Here and now is only a small part of true Life, though. These temptations are strong. That's why "Lead us not into temptation..." is a part of the prayer Jesus taught His disciples. He wanted their focus on the eternal - on true Life, on Him.

Each day we have a choice. Will today be a 'fade to black' day for you? Will you end it glad of the oblivion of sleep? Or will it be a 'fade to Light' day? Will you end it resting in God's strong embrace, glad you're growing closer to Christ as you live each day?

The amazing thing is, **no matter how many times you have chosen a 'fade to black'** existence, Christ still waits to offer you Light - eternal Light. What will tomorrow's decision be?

Reflections

Describe in your own words what a "fade to black" life would be like.

Describe in your own words what a "fade to Light" life would be like.

Which is your life more like? Think about areas of your life in which you could let more of Christ's Light in......

6

Spirit-Showers

No one, when tempted, should say, "I am being tempted by God"; for God cannot be tempted by evil and he himself tempts no one. But one is tempted by one's own desire, being lured and enticed by it; then, when that desire has conceived, it gives birth to sin, and that sin, when it is fully grown, gives birth to death.

Do not be deceived, my beloved. Every generous act of giving, with every perfect gift, is from above, coming down from the Father of lights, with whom there is no variation or shadow due to change. In fulfillment of his own purpose he gave us birth by the word of truth, so that we would become a kind of first fruits of his creatures.

– James 1: 13-18 (New Revised Standard Version)

And remember, no one who wants to do wrong should ever say, "God is tempting me." God is never tempted to do wrong, and he never tempts anyone else either. Temptation comes from the lure of our own evil desires. These evil desires lead to evil actions, and evil actions lead to death.

So don't be misled, my dear brothers and sisters. Whatever is good and perfect comes to us from God above, who created all heaven's lights. Unlike them, he never changes or casts shifting shadows. In his goodness he chose to make us his own children by giving us his true word. And we, out of all creation, became his choice possession.

– James 1: 13-18 (New Living Translation)

* * * * * * * * *

"I'm tired of trying to be something I'm not, but the thing is, I'm not so sure any more just what it is I'm supposed to be!" This was just one reaction to a part of the seminar called A Passionate Life, designed by Walt Kallestad and Mike Breen. This particular week's focus was on discerning one's spiritual gifts, that ministry for which God had uniquely created each of us. As we continued to read and discuss, a visual image related in the readings caught our imagination: It's **like "standing under a bucket of God's grace".** That's when you know you're in your God-created element, living into and using the unique gifts and talents God created you with.

"Wow. **I could really handle a whole bucketful of God's grace falling on me right now!"** This was the same woman's response after reading this image in the A Passionate Life booklet. That began a discussion of what it felt like to try to be something God didn't create us to be. Pretty soon we don't know what we're supposed to be doing. We lose track. We move farther and farther from that awesome cascade of grace falling on us, strengthening us and blessing us.

God creates us in community for times just like these. As we walk this life together, we are **called to be mirrors for one another,** helping each other see the grace-filled gifts and talents we are all created with.

Sometimes we get so far away from God's purpose for our lives that we truly feel tested by God (and many times that we've failed). This Scripture reminds us that God is not the Tempter! No, indeed, it is God who is coaxing and leading us toward that special purpose and life-calling for which He has created us!

So how do you know? Out of all the possibilities that bombard us each day, how do we know which are from God? **Where do we belong?** Many times we find out by trial and error. That means we try it out. Do we feel God's grace falling on us as we make the choice - or do we just feel, well......TRIED?

Where is God pouring grace in your life right now? Where are the "spirit-showers" refreshing your soul? Just like plants, whose roots grow toward water, we too will find growth and fruitful living moving toward and under those bucketfuls of grace!

May God richly bless and lead you as you continue on your life's journey, and may you live each day under the shower of God's grace - by the bucketful!

Reflections

How can you tell when you are "standing under God's grace-showers"?

What is it like when you're not?

Name a place in your life where you feel God's grace right now.

How do you discern where God is calling you to be, and what God is calling you to do?

7

In One Ear and....

"My dear friends, you should be quick to listen and slow to speak or get angry. If you are angry, you cannot do any of the good things that God wants done. You must stop doing anything immoral or evil. Instead be humble and accept the message that is planted in you to save you.

Obey God's message! Don't fool yourself by just listening to it. **If you hear the message and don't obey it, you are like people who stare at themselves in the mirror and forget what they look like as soon as they leave.** *But you must never stop looking at the perfect law that sets you free.* **God will bless you in everything you do, if you listen and obey, and don't just hear and forget.**

If you think you are being religious, but can't control your tongue, you are fooling yourself, and everything you do is useless. Religion that pleases God the Father must be pure and spotless. You must help needy orphans and widows and not let this world make you evil."
- James 1: 19-27 (Contemporary English Version)

"Post this at all the intersections, dear friends: Lead with your ears, follow up with your tongue, and let anger straggle along at the rear. God's righteousness doesn't grow from human anger. So throw all spoiled virtue and cancerous evil in the garbage. **In simple humility, let our gardener, God, landscape you with the Word, making a salvation-garden of your life.**

Don't fool yourself into thinking you are a listener when you are anything but, letting the Word go in one ear and out the other. <u>Act</u> **on what you hear! Those who hear and don't act are like those who glance in the mirror, walk away, and two minutes later have no idea who they are, what they look like.**

But whoever catches a glimpse of the revealed counsel of God – the free life! – even out of the corner of his eye, and sticks with it, is no distracted scatterbrain but a man or woman of action. That person will find delight and affirmation in the action.

Anyone who sets himself up as "religious" by talking a good game is self-deceived. His kind of religion is hot air and only hot air. Real religion, the kind that passes muster before God the Father, is this: Reach out to the homeless and loveless in their plight, and guard against corruption from the godless world."
- James 1: 19-27 (The Message Version)

* * * * * * * * * *

"I'm never going to get this! I'm never going to pass algebra, either!" Arriving at youth group late, Toby slammed his books down on the table. "I just have to pass the stupid test. Then I can forget all this.....stuff!"

20

I began to answer him, but barely got breath drawn and my mouth open when he went on. **"I know, I know. 'You're going to use this one day.'** For what? To torture some other helpless person? Not!"

One of the other youth put a bowl of fresh-popped corn in front of Toby. Good choice. He devoured a few mouthfuls, taking out some (I hoped) of his frustration on the crunchy popcorn. "This is my second time with this....stuff! You'd think I could at least remember it long enough, get it good enough, to pass the stupid class!"

Just then Steve walked in. Think math whiz, guy destined to be an engineer, architect, something very math-y, and you've got the picture. "What's up, Toby? You look a little jazzed - that algebra getting to you again?"

"Getting to me? GETTING to me? Yeah, I guess you could say that. I look at it, stare at it, and mess with it. Then I walk away and 'boom!' I forget everything I just did! **In one ear and out the other!"**

Steve thought a minute. **"Remember what you told me** when I first started coming here? **When I decided this Jesus was for real?** Do you remember that?" Seeing Toby's blank stare, he got his answer. "Well, I remember SOMEONE (grin) talking to me about getting Jesus 'under my skin'. That SOMEONE told me to let Jesus into each part of my life, to relate Him to stuff that was real to me. Remember that, TOBY?" (another grin)

Now Toby really looked puzzled. "I hear you, and I remember. **But I'm already letting Jesus into this.** You wouldn't believe how much I'm praying about this!" Steve just raised his eyebrows and waited, chuckling as a look of understanding began to spread across his friend's face. "OK Steve. Maybe I get it. You mean I should try to relate this algebra....stuff.... to my everyday life so it makes sense, right?" Steve nodded, his smile spreading. "But Jesus is so much easier...."

Now Steve began to laugh. "Maybe for you, but..." He couldn't stop laughing. He couldn't talk, as a belly laugh overtook him: a double-over, tears-in-the-eyes laugh that Toby couldn't help responding to. "Yeah, OK. I remember now. **You couldn't see what use Jesus was outside of a church."** Steve wound down to a big smile. "Yep, and SOMEONE walked with me and helped me relate to Him in my real life. **I bet I can do the same for you with this algebra**, as you say...stuff! Want to give it a try?"

Later, as Steve looked back on his time helping Toby 'get algebra', as he put it, he realized that God was calling him to be a math teacher. **God used Toby to show Steve just how he was uniquely gifted to be,** as he called it, a 'math minister'. Now when Steve looked in the mirror, he saw himself - and Jesus. He recognized in his life the Scripture...
"God will bless you in everything you do, if you listen and obey, and don't just hear and forget."
"But whoever catches a glimpse of the revealed counsel of God – the free life! – even out of the corner of his eye, and sticks with it, is no distracted scatterbrain but a man or woman of action. That person will find delight and affirmation in the action."

✳ ✳ ✳ ✳ ✳ ✳ ✳ ✳ ✳

Toby and his algebra. Steve and living his faith in Jesus. Us and....? **Discovering the Good News of Christ is just the first step.** James tells us that it's in "sticking with it" that we'll find true, deep, everlasting joy. In fact, if we listen and obey, letting Him into each part of our lives, "God will bless us in everything we do", and we'll "find delight and affirmation in the action."

So what about those times, like Toby's, when we definitely are not finding 'delight and affirmation' and 'blessing' in everything we do? Could it be that we're not letting Jesus soak into some areas of our lives?

Sticking with Jesus means letting Him into more and more parts of our lives. It's a lifelong process, a lifelong project. **"In one ear and....."** **NOT out the other**, but soaking into our lives, deeper and deeper!

Reflections

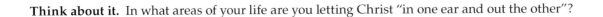

Think about it. In what areas of your life are you letting Christ "in one ear and out the other"?

What would it be like to feel more blessed, more connected to God, each day of your life?

Can you imagine it: the Holy Spirit energy, direction, and focus - in YOUR life?
How would that change your life?

What steps will you take today, this week, this month, to let more of Jesus into your real, everyday life?

8

Abnormal Invitations

My dear brothers and sisters, how can you claim that you have faith in our glorious Lord Jesus Christ if you favor some people more than others? For instance, suppose someone comes into your meeting dressed in fancy clothes and expensive jewelry, and another comes in who is poor and dressed in shabby clothes.

If you give special attention and a good seat to the rich person, but you say to the poor one, "You can stand over there, or else sit on the floor"-- well, doesn't this discrimination show that you are guided by wrong motives?

Listen to me, dear brothers and sisters. Hasn't God chosen the poor in this world to be rich in faith? Aren't they the ones who will inherit the Kingdom he promised to those who love him? And yet, you insult the poor man! Isn't it the rich who oppress you and drag you into court? Aren't they the ones who slander Jesus Christ, whose noble name you bear?

Yes indeed, it is good when you truly obey our Lord's royal command found in the Scriptures: **"Love your neighbor as yourself."** But if you pay special attention to the rich, you are committing a sin, for you are guilty of breaking that law. And **the person who keeps all of the laws except one is as guilty as the person who has broken all of God's laws.** For the same God who said, "Do not commit adultery," also said, "Do not murder." So if you murder someone, you have broken the entire law, even if you do not commit adultery.

So whenever you speak, or whatever you do, remember that **you will be judged by the law of love, the law that sets you free.** For there will be no mercy for you if you have not been merciful to others. But **if you have been merciful, then God's mercy toward you will win out over his judgment against you.**

- James 2: 1-13 (New Living Translation)

My dear friends, don't let public opinion influence how you live out our glorious, Christ-originated faith. If a man enters your church wearing an expensive suit, and a street person wearing rags comes in right after him, and you say to the man in the suit, 'Sit here, sir; this is the best seat in the house!' and either ignore the street person or say, "Better sit here in the back row," haven't you segregated God's children and proved that you are judges who can't be trusted?

Listen, dear friends. **Isn't it clear by now that God operates quite differently?** He chose the world's down-and-out as the kingdom's first citizens, with full rights and privileges. This kingdom is promised to anyone who loves God. And here you are abusing these same citizens! Isn't it the high and mighty who exploit you, who use the courts to rob you blind? Aren't they the ones who scorn the new name – "Christian" – used in your baptisms?

You do well when you complete the Royal Rule of the Scriptures: **"Love others as you love yourself."** But if you play up to these so-called important people, you go against the Rule and stand convicted by it. **You can't pick and** *choose in these things, specializing in keeping one or two things in God's law and ignoring others.* The same God who said, "Don't commit adultery", also said, Don't murder." If you don't commit adultery but go ahead and murder, do you think your non-adultery will cancel out your murder? No, you're a murderer, period.

Talk and act like a person expecting to be judged by the Rule that sets us free. For **if you refuse to act kindly, you can hardly expect to be treated kindly.** Kind mercy wins over harsh judgment every time.

- James 2: 1-13 (The Message Version)

* * * * * * * * * *

It was the most interesting class set-up I'd ever seen. No desks. No chairs. Not even a teacher's desk! Only two things in the classroom the first day: a podium and a big stack of small, sample rugs, each one large enough for one person to sit or stand on.

Well, it WAS a class in abnormal psychology, but....

So we all stood around wondering. **Were we in the right place?** The board did have the correct class title on it, along with the right day and time. So we waited. Some of us began visiting with each other as we waited. Soon there were twenty or thirty of us in the small (and seemingly getting smaller) room.

A bell began to ring from a corner of the room. We quieted down, many of us straining to see who was trying to get our attention. Was it the instructor? Good! Maybe now we'd find out what this weird set-up was all about!

"Welcome to abnormal psychology!" *Ah, there he is, that little short guy - he's the bell-ringer.* A small clearing formed around him and he smiled as he saw many surprised faces. Standing at barely four feet tall, Mr. Palmer addressed us. *Such a big deep voice for such a little man!*

"OK, here's your first assignment. Set your stuff down somewhere out of the way. Then look around. **Find the person you think is the most different from yourself** and list ten things that are different about you. You've got ten minutes. Go!!"

All righty then. Now **this might have been easy if** I was really short, really tall, had purple hair,... or something. But there I was, five foot seven, not fat, not thin, no purple hair *(drat - that would have made this assignment SO much easier!)* Maybe if I moved to the edge, the outside of the crowd in the middle of the room.......

And there he was! Hunkered down in the corner, watching the action, was a man with the most lively, mischievous eyes I'd ever seen. I scooted and tripped around elbows, feet, and the myriad of book bags and coats strung out along the wall until I reached him. "Hi, I'm Al." He pointed at his own chest. "Cal", he announced, in a strange, interestingly muted voice.

As I began to talk, I noticed that those lively eyes were fixed...on my mouth. Cal whipped a small notebook out of his pocket and wrote quickly. "I'm deaf, and I don't talk so well...didn't catch what we're supposed to be doing." I read and understood. "Well," I began, "we're supposed to find someone we think is the most different from us and then figure out ten ways we're different."

Confusion entered his eyes for a split second, then the most infectious laughter bubbled out of him. He scribbled on his pad: "I'm deaf. How about you?" "Nope, not me!" I countered, "I'm female, how about you?" Now we were having a great time, and some folks around us had stopped to listen in. Cal was laughing so hard his pencil shook as he wrote. "Nope, I'm a guy all the way. Hey, there's a letter difference in our names: Al...Cal. How about that?" And so it went. **Soon the bell rang again.**

We were instructed to grab one of the rugs and place it anywhere in the room. Mr. Palmer announced. "It'll be your 'home base' for the rest of class. Three minutes: go!" Predictably, many of us chose to put our 'home bases' next to the person we'd just finished talking to.

Then came the challenge. "Think about this: you're having a party, a really special get-together. You're deciding who to invite. The only rule is **you must invite the person who's the most different from you - the one you just talked to.** Think hard, and be honest with yourself. Who else would you invite? More importantly, who would you hesitate to invite? Who wouldn't you invite at all? Oh, by the way, I may be short, but I know human nature. Some of you thought I wouldn't notice you chatting away with people so much like you, you could be sisters or brothers! Ten minutes - go!"

Silence descended over the room as minds scrambled. Paper and pens were passed around as we all thought about what Mr. Palmer had just said. Soon, you guessed it, that irritating **bell rang again.**

"OK, three minutes to write today's assignment. Name and date at the top please. Now, write down three reasons TO invite your conversation partner to your party and three reasons NOT to invite them." A hand instantly shot up. **"But, but.....don't you mean** which of our friends we'd invite and not invite.....sir?" A big smile spread across Mr. Palmer's face.

"Nope. **Welcome to real-world psychology. The real question isn't your friends. It's you. Who is included - and excluded - in your world, and why?"**

* * * * * * * * *

*"My dear friends, don't let public opinion influence how you live out our glorious, Christ-originated faith ..... **Isn't it clear by now that God operates quite differently?** ....So whenever you speak, or whatever you do, remember that you will be judged by the law of love, the law that sets you free."*

We're human. We naturally gravitate to, and include in our world, others who are like us. A friend once called that **'personal public opinion'.** It's like taking a poll to check out the advantages and disadvantages of being seen with another person. **"What will people think?",** we often ask ourselves (even if subconsciously).

God is a God of inclusion, not exclusion. Jesus didn't just chat informally with 'that' kind of people - you know, the ones who'd never make most invitation lists. No. He operated quite differently. Tax collectors. Prostitutes. You could add a few, I'm sure. And He didn't just chat briefly and then move on, either. He actually...ATE with them!

Shift the focus a minute. **Who wouldn't invite you to a party?** Why not? Doesn't it feel good to know that no matter what, Jesus would invite you to His party, His dinner, His Table? In fact, Jesus invites you each and every week to share a meal with Him, to spend time with Him, and to be loved by Him.

Jesus, our eternal Host, the One who judges not on exclusion and difference, not on past mistakes, but judges using the..."law of love, which sets us free."
As we follow Him, what are our invitations based on? Are we willing to be judged the same way we judge others? To be invited the same way we invite others?

Remember, **what the world might see as 'abnormal'** is perfectly normal to God, because He does indeed "operate quite differently". Praise God for that!!

Reflections

What kinds of people is it the easiest for you to include in your life? The hardest?

How has God sent people into your life to stretch your spirit of invitation and inclusion?

How have you responded?

Think of the groups you belong to (friends, family, clubs, church, regular gatherings, etc.).
How inclusive and/or exclusive are they? Why do you think this is?

Have you ever gone someplace new and different? How was that?

Have you ever invited someone to a group or family event that was a little "different"? How was that?

9

Seamless Faith

What good is it, my brothers and sisters, if you say you have faith but do not have works? Can faith save you? If a brother or sister is naked and lacks daily food, and one of you says to them, "Go in peace; keep warm and eat your fill," and yet you do not supply their bodily needs, what is the good of that? So faith by itself, if it has no works, is dead.

But someone will say, "You have faith and I have works." Show me your faith apart from your works, and I by my works will show you my faith.

You believe that God is one; you do well. Even the demons believe-- and shudder. Do you want to be shown, you senseless person, that faith apart from works is barren? Was not our ancestor Abraham justified by works when he offered his son Isaac on the altar? You see that faith was active along with his works, and faith was brought to completion by the works. Thus the scripture was fulfilled that says, "Abraham believed God, and it was reckoned to him as righteousness," and he was called the friend of God.

You see that a person is justified by works and not by faith alone. Likewise, was not Rahab the prostitute also justified by works when she welcomed the messengers and sent them out by another road? *For just as the body without the spirit is dead, so faith without works is also dead.*

- James 2: 14-26 (New Revised Standard Version)

My friends, what good is it to say you have faith, when you don't do anything to show that you really do have faith? Can that kind of faith save you? If you know someone who doesn't have any clothes or food, you shouldn't just say, "I hope all goes well for you. I hope you will be warm and have plenty to eat." Faith that doesn't lead us to do good deeds is all alone and dead!

Suppose someone disagrees and says, "It is possible to have faith without doing kind deeds." I would answer, "Prove that you have faith without doing kind deeds, and I will prove that I have faith by doing them." You surely believe there is only one God. That's fine. Even demons believe this, and it makes them shake with fear.

Does some stupid person want proof that faith without deeds is useless? Well, our ancestor Abraham pleased God by putting his son Isaac on the altar to sacrifice him. Now you see how Abraham's faith and deeds worked together. He proved that his faith was real by what he did. This is what the Scriptures mean by saying, "Abraham had faith in God, and God was pleased with him." That's how Abraham became God's friend.

You can now see that we please God by what we do and not only by what we believe. For example, Rahab had been a prostitute. But she pleased God when she welcomed the spies and sent them home by another way. *Anyone who doesn't breathe is dead, and faith that doesn't do anything is just as dead!*

- James 2: 14-26 (Contemporary English Version)

* * * * * * * * *

Ever since she was a little girl watching her grandmother sew beautiful clothes, Samantha had dreamed of the day she could add "Tailor" behind her name. She'd even designed her future business cards. **But today was one of those days.** Her dad had called them "the days that separate fantasy from reality and connect dreams with hard work".

Today was the day Samantha had to pass the "seamless collar" test. She had to apply a seamless turtleneck collar to a shirt. No wrinkles. No pleats. No uneven edges. It was one of the many requirements she had to achieve to pass her tailoring class. In fact, it was the last test she had to pass to complete the course.

Memories of bragging to her cousin over coffee that morning came back to her. "Piece of cake!" she'd boldly said then. *Yeah, right. What WAS I thinking?* Her cousin Mort thought safety pins and duct tape (well hidden, of course) constituted the only clothing skills one really needed. Tailoring, well, in his opinion it was only for the rich and famous. His question had intrigued her though. **"Just how do they make seamless collars anyway?",** he'd asked her. "I mean really, Sam, they have to begin and end somewhere, don't they?" Samantha hadn't a clue. All she cared about was getting one - just one - of them perfectly applied to a shirt.

Now on her fifth try, she was beginning to wish she'd never bragged to Mort about how easy it was. **Just then she noticed Seeya watching her** with her kind, caring eyes. Seeya always had kind eyes - for everyone, even the crabby old delivery man who brought tailoring supplies every week. Not a word of English, but her eyes spoke volumes.

Just as Samantha was about to totally lose patience (and all hope of success), Seeya rolled her chair over next to her. Reaching over to the supply table, Seeya picked up two shirts and two seamless collars. Handing one set to Samantha, she began, step-by-step, to guide Samantha through the process.

It wasn't until a gleeful and triumphant Samantha finally got that collar sewn on (no wrinkles, no folds, smooth as ever!) that she looked over at Seeya's clean and tidy table and realized she'd finished with all her requirements hours ago. Seeya's completed course checklist was the only thing on her sewing table besides the neatly packed box of school supplies.

"Why did you stay?", Samantha tried to ask in her best sign language. Seeya responded with a bright smile. Motioning 'sleep' with her hands, and pointing to her head to demonstrate 'dreams', she followed up with showing muscles to represent 'hard work'. **Dreams and hard work. Samantha's bragging and reality.** As she hugged Seeya and tearfully said a goodbye she realized two things. First, she'd never really paid much attention to Seeya. Second, she realized Seeya only had one set of clothes: white shirt and black slacks. Funny how she'd never realized that, even with all the attention she gave to sewing, fabric, and clothing these last months.

As she watched Seeya leave, **Samantha realized she prayed for poor people every Sunday** in church - it was part of the church service every week! Funny how she'd never connected those prayers with actual people, never thought about what she could do.

As she packed up her own supplies and prepared to go home, Samantha remembered something - Seeya had served as the clothing sizing model for their class! **She stopped by the instructor's office on the way out.** Mrs. Jin looked up as Samantha peeked in. "Can I help you? I noticed you got the last thing done - congratulations!" "Thanks, but I was wondering. Was Seeya the sizing model for all the women's clothes we made?" A warm smile spread across the instructor's face. "Why yes, she was. It's how she paid her tuition. Why do you ask?"

"Well, did you notice she always wears the same clothes? I was just wondering, well,... if maybe..... Could she just have the clothes? I mean then she'd have some choices. I could pay for them..." Samantha didn't know what else to say.

Mrs. Jin seemed deep in thought, staring out the small window of her office. Samantha waited. Finally, she looked up. **"How does fifty dollars sound?",** she asked. "Fifty dollars? For a whole wardrobe?" A very surprised **Seeya received a visit from the "crabby old delivery man"** that evening.

Funny thing, though, **he didn't look so crabby when** he saw Seeya's astonished joy as he carried five boxes into her rented room. "For me?", she motioned. "Yep," the delivery man nodded. And you know what? He just couldn't keep a straight face. Before he knew it he was smiling - a big, bold, light-up-the-room kind of smile. As he left, there was a new bounce in his step and new life in his face. *Maybe, just maybe, some of those Christians weren't all talk after all. Maybe some of them were for real. Wonder what church that girl Samantha goes to?* A new sense of hope trickled into his mind as he drove home that night.

* * * * * * * * *

Seamless collars, just flowing all the way around the neckline of those turtlenecks. Connecting smoothly: no wrinkles, no pleats, no glitches.

Seamless faith. Words flowing into real life action, connecting smoothly - just like they belong together - because they do.

Just like a shirt isn't a shirt without a collar, a collar would look pretty silly (and perhaps a bit scandalous) if worn without the rest of the shirt, so our words of faith are vastly incomplete without matching actions. Actions without purposeful faith grounding them aren't really complete either.

As James says so well, *"My friends, what good is it to say you have faith, when you don't do anything to show that you really do have faith?"* Just like Samantha tried many times before she got that collar right, so we try many times in life to make our faith and actions go together. It's often called "walking our talk" of faith. As we grow and mature in our life's journey as Christ's disciples, we are challenged to "walk our talk" with more and more success, spreading the reality of His Good News in a real world full of people like that delivery man who have seen so much "empty faith" that they have almost lost hope. Almost.

Reflections

You can be an instrument of hope - yes, YOU! How might that work out in your real everyday life?

Think about that delivery man. How can Christ touch others through you this week in your work or school life?

Think of a time in your life when you have been unexpectedly touched by grace, perhaps as Seeya was. Describe how it affected you.

How would you describe "seamless faith"?

10

Open Mouth, Insert....

Dear brothers and sisters, not many of you should become teachers in the church, for we who teach will be judged by God with greater strictness. We all make many mistakes, but those who control their tongues can also control themselves in every other way.

We can make a large horse turn around and go wherever we want by means of a small bit in its mouth. **And a tiny rudder makes a huge ship turn wherever the pilot wants it to go, even though the winds are strong.** *So also, the tongue is a small thing, but what enormous damage it can do. A tiny spark can set a great forest on fire.* **And the tongue is a flame of fire.** *It is full of wickedness that can ruin your whole life.* **It can turn the entire course of your life into a blazing flame of destruction, for it is set on fire by hell itself.**

People can tame all kinds of animals and birds and reptiles and fish, but no one can tame the tongue. It is an uncontrollable evil, full of deadly poison. Sometimes it praises our Lord and Father, and sometimes it breaks out into curses against those who have been made in the image of God. And so blessing and cursing come pouring out of the same mouth. Surely, my brothers and sisters, this is not right!

Does a spring of water bubble out with both fresh water and bitter water? Can you pick olives from a fig tree or figs from a grapevine? No, and you can't draw fresh water from a salty pool.

- James 3: 1-12 (New Living Translation)

Don't be in any rush to become a teacher, my friends. Teaching is highly responsible work. Teachers are held to the strictest standards. And none of us is perfectly qualified. We get it wrong nearly every time we open our mouths. If you could find someone whose speech was perfectly true, you'd have a perfect person, in perfect control of life.

A bit in the mouth of a horse controls the whole horse. **A small rudder on a huge ship in the hands of a skilled captain sets a course in the face of the strongest winds. A word out of your mouth may seem of no account, but it can accomplish nearly anything – or destroy it!**

It only takes a spark, remember, to set off a forest fire. A careless or wrongly placed word out of your mouth can do that. **By our speech we can ruin the world, turn harmony to chaos, throw mud on a reputation, send the whole world up in smoke and go up in smoke with it, smoke right from the pit of hell.**

This is scary: You can tame a tiger, but you can't tame a tongue – it's never been done. The tongue runs wild, a wanton killer. With our tongues we bless God our Father; with the same tongues we curse the very men and women he made in his image. Curses and blessings out of the same mouth!

My friends, this can't go on. A spring doesn't gush fresh water one day and brackish water the next, does it? Apple trees don't bear strawberries, do they? Raspberry bushes don't bear apples, do they? You're not going to dip into a polluted mud hole and get a cup of clear, cool water, are you?

- James 3: 1-12 (The Message Version)

✳ ✳ ✳ ✳ ✳ ✳ ✳ ✳ ✳

Ed saw his friend Stan at the local hardware store. **"Hey Stan, did you hear?** Bob's going to start working as a greeter at WalMart. It should help him pay off Margaret's medical bills. He's real happy - looks better than I've seen him since she died last year. I'm so glad he came in and applied. I figured it was the least I could do for him, being's I'm the personnel guy, you know?"

Stan leaned in close to Ed. **"Well, I shouldn't really say this, but** did you know he did drugs back in high school? Really. He went through jobs like water too. And you should know he took five bucks from the concession stand cash register back then too."

High school? Is he really listening to what he's saying? "You know, Stan, that was a very long time ago. Good thing I've known Bob over forty years now; **you know words like that can ruin a man, don't you?"**

Open mouth, insert foot.
"...the tongue is a small thing, but what enormous damage it can do. A tiny spark can set a great forest on fire. And the tongue is a flame of fire. It is full of wickedness that can ruin your whole life."

✳ ✳ ✳ ✳ ✳ ✳ ✳ ✳ ✳

Sue called her friend Tammy the instant she heard the news about Erin's pregnancy. "She told me not to tell anyone else, but.....it's really not her first baby, because she gave her first baby up for adoption. I bet nobody knows that, either..."

Tammy had no patience for gossip, and frankly she was shocked to hear it coming from Sue. *Was this the same Sue who complained that other people talked about her?*

"Yeah, I bet nobody knows. **I don't even think her husband knows!"** Tammy cringed at the conspiring gleam in Sue's green eyes. *Anyone else? What did Sue think Erin meant, she wanted to tell the world?*

"You know what, Sue? Did you ever think that maybe Erin didn't want 'anyone else' to know? Maybe she should be able to decide who <u>she</u> wants to tell - and when. I mean, it's not like she's wanted for bank robbery or something. Erin gave a family a huge gift back then. What kind of a gift are you giving her?"

Open mouth, insert foot.
"...By our speech we can ruin the world, turn harmony to chaos, throw mud on a reputation, ..."

✳ ✳ ✳ ✳ ✳ ✳ ✳ ✳ ✳

Ned spotted his boss Tom in line at the local fast food place. "Hey Boss, I heard you're thinking about hiring Phil to do that custom cabinet job. He doesn't like to talk about himself much, but Phil does awesome work. You know Carl, right? Well, call Carl if you want details, but don't let Phil know I told you how good he is, OK? Here's Carl's business card."

A few days later, Phil pulled up in line behind Ned at the gas station. "Hey Ned, you don't happen to know how Tom got hold of Carl, do you? Mmm hmmm. I thought so. You're something else. Don't know how I ever deserved great friends like you. Anyway, I got the job - my dream job. Never thought I'd land one like it, and I start Monday. Thanks, bro!"

Open mouth, insert grace.
"...A word out of your mouth may seem of no account, but it can accomplish nearly anything ..."

* * * * * * * * * *

Jen called Shelly right after she finished talking to Paula. "She's so excited. They've been trying for three years to have a baby. I know Paula wants to wait before she tells too many people, but **she said I could tell you - just you.** I was thinking, well, you and I should start planning a baby shower for later on. If we start planning now, then later when she wants to tell people we'll be ready for the best baby shower ever!"

Shelly could hardly contain herself, she was so thrilled. "But Jen, we should tell Sally, and Melanie, and Pam would want to know, and...."

"Whoa! No <u>way</u>! **Didn't you hear what I just said?** It's not about us. It's about Paula, Cole, and their family-to-be. She said <u>only</u> us. Got it?"

Shelly stopped and thought. Jen was right (as usual about stuff like this). "OK, I guess you're right, Jen. I just got a bit carried away, that's all. In fact, I <u>know</u> you're right. It'll be our secret - and what fun we'll have planning!"

Open mouth, insert grace.
"...A word out of your mouth may seem of no account, but it can accomplish nearly anything ..."

* * * * * * * * * *

Amazing what words can do, isn't it? Once they're out, they're impossible to take back. We often think of this fact in negative terms ("open mouth, insert foot").

How about turning our thinking around? How can we give control of our tongues to the Holy Spirit more every day? How can we get our tongues in WWJD habit - "walk with Jesus daily"?

If we are truly on a life journey of discipleship to Jesus, the Christ, and we claim Him as our Lord and <u>Savior</u>, **will we let Him save our tongues too?**

Reflections

How can we react in a Christ-like way when others let their tongues get out of control, like in these real-life stories?

How can you use your tongue today as God's instrument of grace and blessing?

11

Wisdom Seeds

Are any of you wise or sensible? Then show it by living right and by being humble and wise in everything you do. *But if your heart is full of bitter jealousy and selfishness, don't brag or lie to cover up the truth. That kind of wisdom doesn't come from above. It is earthly and selfish and comes from the devil himself.*

Whenever people are jealous or selfish, they cause trouble and do all sorts of cruel things. But the wisdom that comes from above leads us to be pure, friendly, gentle, sensible, kind, helpful, genuine, and sincere. *When peacemakers plant seeds of peace, they will harvest justice.*

- James 3: 13-18 (Contemporary English Version)

If you are wise and understand God's ways, live a life of steady goodness so that only good deeds will pour forth. *And if you don't brag about the good you do, then you will be truly wise!*

But if you are bitterly jealous and there is selfish ambition in your hearts, don't brag about being wise. That is the worst kind of lie. For jealousy and selfishness are not God's kind of wisdom. Such things are earthly, unspiritual, and motivated by the Devil. For wherever there is jealousy and selfish ambition, there you will find disorder and every kind of evil.

But the wisdom that comes from heaven is first of all pure. It is also peace loving, gentle at all times, and willing to yield to others. It is full of mercy and good deeds. It shows no partiality and is always sincere. *And those who are peacemakers will plant seeds of peace and reap a harvest of goodness.*

- James 3: 13-18 (New Living Translation)

* * * * * * * * *

Five year old Bradley (Brad to his buddies) sat in the doctor's office waiting room... waiting. Bo-o-o-ring! He'd already read all the kids magazines and looked at the toys (definitely baby stuff), so he sat, dangling his legs off the edge of the chair, kicking his shoes together. Bo-o-o-ring. **When would it be THEIR turn?** His mom sat next to him, his new little brother in the baby carrier snoozing. *Boy, that's the life, sleep when you want, get fed, and you don't even have to walk anyplace!* It <u>was</u> pretty cool having a baby brother, though.

"Mrs. Rivers?" The nurse peeked out and called his mom's name. "Mrs. Rivers, he'll be fine out here. We'll keep an eye on him, OK?" Mom looked at Bradley. He puffed his chest up and smiled back. **"I'm a big boy**

now, Mom. I'm good." With that announcement, mom and baby went through the door to see the doctor. *Whew! That was a close one!* The farther Bradley stayed away from doctors and needles, the better he felt.

Just a minute later the outside office door opened and **in came a boy just about Bradley's age.** *Whoo-hoo! A new friend!* Right behind the boy was his mom, and wow, was her tummy big! Bradley spoke right up. **"Hey, I'm Brad. Looks like you're gonna have a baby brother** real soon!" Friendly eyes and a big smile answered his greeting. **"I'm BJ, and we're having a baby... sister."** He slid closer to Bradley and dropped his voice to a whisper. "Wish it WAS a brother though. **How'm I gonna play with a...girl?"**

BJ's mom checked in at the counter, and **soon BJ and Brad were sitting together** at the kids' table. The boys discovered they were both in kindergarten, and liked to play soccer. Brad told BJ about his new baby brother. **"He's six weeks old today** - that's almost two whole months!" BJ wrinkled his forehead. "Do you get to play with him yet?", he asked. "I mean, **does he like trucks, or t-ball, or soccer or anything?"**

"Um...not quite. I make funny faces at him and tickle his feet and stuff like that." BJ didn't look like he was too thrilled about this whole new baby thing. Sensing that he had an expert to ask all his questions to, he took a big breath. **"So Brad, what DO you do with a baby? At least you've got a new brother. I get a.....girl!"**

"Well, my mom only told me one thing, but sometimes it's real hard, and I think it'll get harder once Timmy gets bigger, **'cause my friend Michael says HIS baby brother eats his toys!"**

Now BJ was getting worried. "Ewww!" What about his new Transformers? Would it be like when they got the new puppy last year and it ate some of the new building set he got for his birthday?

"I don't know about that yet, but mom says my baby brother Timmy'll do what I do, 'cause I'm the big brother. So if I fight and get all mean, then he will too. **She says I have to plant 'nice wisdom seeds', so he'll learn to be nice and act smart.** It's pretty easy now, 'cause all I have to do now is try to be gentle and talk nice to him. **But if Timmy tries to eat my toys,** those 'nice wisdom seeds' of mom's are gonna be a lot harder to plant!"

* * * * * * * * *

A life of 'steady goodness'.
Live right and be humble in all you do. *All? Now that's a pretty tall order!*
Plant seeds of peace and harvest goodness and justice.

Even when life seems to be 'eating your toys'?
Even when your life, like young Brad's and BJ's, gets unpredictable?
Even when......(what would you put here?).

Yes, even then.

Brad changed BJ's whole outlook. BJ's mom couldn't figure it out at first. BJ went from begging his mom to **trade the baby in for a brother, or maybe a puppy,**...(anything but a SISTER) to planning how he could play with his new sister when she arrived. "Can I make funny faces and tickle her feet when she gets here?", he'd asked when his mom came out of the doctor's office. *What?* She almost looked around to be sure she'd picked up the right boy!

"Hey mom, this is Brad. He's my new friend. He's a new big brother, like I'm gonna be. Think our babies can play together? Brad and me, we wanna plant seeds. His mom calls them 'nice wisdom seeds', and I wanna grow some of those plants. Can we, Mom? Can we? Please?"

And that's how two families became best friends. Years later, when Brad married BJ's sister Meghan, BJ's wedding reception toast included a basket of seed packets. Relabeled, they read "Love", Wisdom", "Strength", "Faith". etc. and sat as the centerpiece on the wedding party's table.

Those seeds took Brad and BJ through some tough times.
Even when it seemed that life was truly 'eating their toys'.
Even when life got scary and unpredictable.
Even then.

No, it won't be perfect. It won't be always peaceful and humble and wise.
But seeds of peace do grow a harvest of goodness and justice.
Seeds of love and strength do grow a harvest of a deeply joyful life.
Even, no, **especially in the hard times.**

That's why God created us in community with one another - Brad and BJ, you and I.
Take some time today, maybe even right now, to be thankful for the 'nice wisdom seeds' others have planted in your life.
Take some time today to talk with God. Ask him to show you ways to plant Christ's 'nice wisdom seeds' in the people God places in your life. How about your friends? family? people you meet in passing?

"...the wisdom that comes from above leads us to be pure, friendly, gentle, sensible, kind, helpful, genuine, and sincere."

Couldn't the world use more of these things?
Let's get planting!

Reflections

Describe a time when someone planted "wisdom seeds" in your life? What effect did that have on you?

What would "planting wisdom seeds" look like in your daily life?

12

Which Side?

Those conflicts and disputes among you, where do they come from? Do they not come from your cravings that are at war within you?

You want something and do not have it; so you commit murder. And you covet something and cannot obtain it; so you engage in disputes and conflicts. You do not have, because you do not ask. You ask and do not receive, because you ask wrongly, in order to spend what you get on your pleasures. Adulterers! Do you not know that friendship with the world is enmity with God? Therefore whoever wishes to be a friend of the world becomes an enemy of God.

Or do you suppose that it is for nothing that the scripture says, "God yearns jealously for the spirit that he has made to dwell in us"? **But he gives all the more grace; therefore it says, "God opposes the proud, but gives grace to the humble."** *Submit yourselves therefore to God. Resist the devil, and he will flee from you.*

Draw near to God, and he will draw near to you. Cleanse your hands, you sinners, and purify your hearts, you double-minded. Lament and mourn and weep. Let your laughter be turned into mourning and your joy into dejection. **Humble yourselves before the Lord, and he will exalt you.**

- James 4: 1-10 (New Revised Standard Version)

Where do you think all these appalling wars and quarrels come from? Do you think they just happen? Think again. They come about because you want your own way, and fight for it deep inside yourselves. You lust for what you don't have and are willing to kill to get it. You want what isn't yours and will risk violence to get your hands on it.

You wouldn't think of just asking God for it, would you? And why not? Because you know you'd be asking for what you have no right to. You're spoiled children, each wanting your own way.

You're cheating on God. If all you want is your own way, flirting with the world every chance you get, you end up enemies of God and his way. And do you suppose God doesn't care? The proverb has it that "he's a fiercely jealous lover." **And what he gives in love is far better than anything else you'll find. It's common knowledge that "God goes against the willful proud; God gives grace to the willing humble."**

So let God work his will in you. Yell a loud no to the Devil and watch him scamper. Say a quiet yes to God and he'll be there in no time. *Quit dabbling in sin. Purify your inner life. Quit playing the field. Hit bottom, and cry your eyes out. The fun and games are over. Get serious, really serious. Get down on your knees before the Master; it's the only way you'll get on your feet.*

- James 4: 1-10 (The Message Version)

* * * * * * * * *

Meghan hated Friday afternoons. They always picked teams and played kickball. **The only thing she hated more than kickball was picking teams.** At ten years old and measuring a full five-foot-ten, sports weren't exactly her favorite way to spend an afternoon (or any time, for that matter). **Her doctor had told her mom just last week he thought Meghan would be well over six feet tall when she was grown up.** *Great, I'll always be a freak*, she thought.

Mr. Jennings, her fifth grade teacher, chose the captains. *Oh great. Delia and Frank.* Meghan sank lower in her chair. **Maybe if she slumped far enough down, no one would notice her.**

Meghan was <u>way</u> tired of being picked last - way, way tired.

What she didn't know was that earlier that day Delia had spotted her own name and Frank's written in Mr. Jennings's lesson plan book on his desk. Delia had let Frank know right away, passing him a note on her way to the trash can. It was short and to the point: **"Hey, you pick Meghan, and I'll give you five bucks."**

Frank smiled - big - for a second. **Meghan.** *Oh yeah, "four feet". Why she's so tall she trips just walking across the room!* **Frank scribbled a quick answer.** Then he got up to "throw away some trash". On his way, he slipped Delia his answer: **"Ten bucks?"** On the way back to his seat, he risked a quick glance back at her over his shoulder as she flashed him a 'OK' sign. He began planning two things. First, how would he spend his new found wealth? Second, and not so easy, **how would he get away with playing Meghan for the least time possible in the kickball game that afternoon.** Left field maybe? Not much action out there, and maybe she'd even trip and skin her knees or something. Yeah, then she'd be out of the game entirely and he'd still have his ten bucks. Hmmm...

The morning went quickly, and soon they were all back in the classroom after lunch. **Team picking time. Meghan sank back down in her seat,** daydreaming about what she'd do after school. She almost missed the surprise. Was she dreaming? **Had Frank just said her name?**

"I said, I'll take....Meghan!" *First, he'd picked her first! Wow!"* She'd never been picked first (or even close to it). She was so surprised and happy that she missed the look of total glee on Delia's face as she got up to stand beside Frank.

As soon as the teams were chosen, the class headed out to the kickball field and the game began. Four innings passed. **With only one inning left in the game, the score was tied six to six.**

Then Delia's team scored a run in the bottom of the fifth. *Oh boy*, Frank thought. *Well, Meghan's seventh in line to kick. Maybe (hopefully) we can score before then...*

But it wasn't to be. **Bases loaded, two outs, and.....here came that seventh kicker to the plate: Meghan. Frank groaned.** The team stared down at the dirt, just knowing what was coming next.

Bam! The kick could be heard all the way out in left field. Meghan stood frozen in place at the plate. *Did I do that?* she thought, as the ball went flying out past the pitcher, past second base, over the head of the tall center fielder, and almost over the fence at the far, far end of the field.

"RUN! Run, Meghan, run!" Mr. Jennings yelled. "You did it, Meghan! Run, girl, run!!" And she did. Her smile was huge as she ran all the way around the bases. She didn't even trip once!
Both teams were stunned (to say the least). It took Frank's team a few seconds to even look up to see their

runners all streaking across home plate. Four runs! Wow! Cheers erupted from Frank's team bench. "Go, Meghan, go!", they all chanted.

Delia couldn't believe her eyes. Meghan? Old "four-feet"? "Thought you said this game was 'in the bag', Delia." She turned to see Bob staring at her. "You owe me, girlie. I bet my buddy Stan over there we'd win - five bucks. Hand it over. This is your fault, you and your 'sure thing'!" Delia reached into her pocket. *Great, just great. All she had was fifteen bucks.*

"Hey troops, I say let's celebrate. I see the ice cream cart over there on the sidewalk. Ice cream's on me for everyone. Let's go!" Mr. Jennings' voice rang out over the cheers, and soon they were all headed for the ice cream cart.

As they were all sitting on the benches by the field, a car pulled past them into the parking lot with a short 'toot' of its horn. **Mr. Jennings waved. "Hey, that's my brother, kids. He teaches for the Peace Corps in South America.** Let's get him an ice cream too!"

Meghan watched as Mr. Jennings' brother unfolded himself from the car. Unfolded was the right word as she and the other kids watched him look taller, and taller, and.....
Frank was the first to ask as his mouth fell open and his eyes opened wide. **"Mr. Jennings, how tall IS your brother?"**

"Oh, Matt there? I think he's about seven foot six now, plus or minus." "Wow", the kids said, almost in unison. Mr. Jennings called out to his brother, "Hey, cloud-man, want an ice cream?" The two men met in a big bear hug as the kids gathered around. **Matt looked at the kids, and he noticed Meghan first.** "Hey, are you the big kicker I saw as I drove in? Good foot on you, girl. Smart team that picked you!" **Meghan stood up a bit straighter.** She couldn't remember the last time she actually felt proud to be....tall.

They all walked back to the school building together. Soon all the kids had left, leaving Mr. Jennings and his brother Matt alone in the classroom. **Matt knew his brother well. "So, big brother, what did I miss?** Knowing you, it looks like your plan came together big, whatever it was."

Mr. Jennings smiled as he packed his school bag. **"Yep. Human nature, that's all.** I wrote these two kids' names in my lesson plan book where I knew they'd snoop and see it. They did all the rest. You know, **I'm glad you showed up when you did.** Meghan, she's been really down on herself because she's so tall. She saw that picture on my desk the other day - the one of you and me, and she told me, '**Mr. J., I keep praying God will shrink me,** you know, make me normal, but He never does. Everything would be so much better if I was shorter. **Then I could do everything I want to. I'd do ANYTHING to shrink,** Mr. J., really I would!' I told her maybe she should try to be the best tall girl she could be. I tried to tell her all the neat things about being tall. Then I remembered all you went through being so tall, and I started praying for her...just like I used to pray for you, little brother."

Matt thought a minute. "You know, I never told you this, but I heard you praying for me, and it changed my life. You probably don't even remember, but I do. You said, 'God, help Matt to go Your way, because You've made him so tall for Your purpose. Help him to find Your way, not just his.' I was twelve, and it was the first day of seventh grade. You changed my life, big brother. **I chose sides that day. I chose God's side, God's purpose.** That's why I'm teaching in the Peace Corps today."

As the two men walked across the parking lot, a voice stopped them. **"Mom! There he is! Mr. Jennings! Mr. Jennings! I want my mom to meet your brother!"** That parking lot conversation began a new relationship.

Meghan's mother was a single mom, and Matt had never thought he'd find a woman who would, as he said "risk a permanent crooked neck looking up all the time" to be with him. A year later, "Matchmaker Meghan", as her mom now called her, served as the maid of honor in her mom's and Matt's wedding.

Meghan, now a six-foot tall sixth-grader, wanted to make a toast at the reception. It was simple. "I just want to say I'm SO glad to have a tall dad! **He's taught me to choose sides - God's side.** We pray together every day, and I think God's got stuff planned for a tall girl like me. Right, Tall-Dad?" And she sat down, glad God had chosen her for His team, and glad she'd chosen God's way for her life.

❊ ❊ ❊ ❊ ❊ ❊ ❊ ❊ ❊

How about us? **Are we glad we're chosen to be on 'God's team'?** How do we show it? Would others know which side we're on? **Are we serious? Are we the "willingly humble", living out of the power of God's grace?**

Are you tempted to think you're too...tall, short, old, young, ... for God to have a purpose for you? What would you have told Meghan? One of the ways we are tempted not to choose "God's side" is when we think we have nothing to offer. Hear God telling you in the middle of those times that you are created in God's image, with God-given purpose, and hear God calling your name out. God has 'picked you' with the gift of His son Jesus!

Or....like Matt, are you tempted to go your own way? Perhaps you think your way is best. You've got it all planned. You know, "Thanks anyway, God. If I get in trouble, I'll call you if I need You, OK?" Yeah, right. Hear the end of this Scripture again: *"Get serious, really serious. Get down on your knees before the Master; it's the only way you'll get on your feet."*

Whatever your obstacle to saying "yes" to being on God's team, Christ can overcome it. He has already chosen you. **Remember, "...***what he gives in love is far better than anything else you'll find."*

Reflections

What would you tell someone who thought they weren't good enough, or gifted enough, or _____ enough for God to have a purpose for them?

What kind of obstacles to serving on "God's team" get in people's way and keep them from serving?

How do we show we're on "God's team" in our daily lives?

13

Haven't You Heard?

Do not speak evil against one another, brothers and sisters. Whoever speaks evil against another or judges another, speaks evil against the law and judges the law; but if you judge the law, you are not a doer of the law but a judge. There is one lawgiver and judge who is able to save and to destroy. So who, then, are you to judge your neighbor?

Come now, you who say, "Today or tomorrow we will go to such and such a town and spend a year there, doing business and making money." Yet you do not even know what tomorrow will bring. What is your life? For you are a mist that appears for a little while and then vanishes.

Instead you ought to say, "If the Lord wishes, we will live and do this or that." As it is, you boast in your arrogance; all such boasting is evil. Anyone, then, who knows the right thing to do and fails to do it, commits sin.

- James 4: 11-17 (New Revised Standard Version)

My friends, don't say cruel things about others! If you do, or if you condemn others, you are condemning God's Law. And if you condemn the Law, you put yourself above the Law and refuse to obey either it or God who gave it. God is our judge, and he can save or destroy us. What right do you have to condemn anyone?

You should know better than to say, "Today or tomorrow we will go to the city. We will do business there for a year and make a lot of money!" What do you know about tomorrow? How can you be so sure about your life? It is nothing more than mist that appears for only a little while before it disappears. You should say, "If the Lord lets us live, we will do these things." Yet you are stupid enough to brag, and it is wrong to be so proud. If you don't do what you know is right, you have sinned.

- James 4: 11-17 (Contemporary English Version)

* * * * * * * * *

"Who made him the boss anyway? If people only knew! Did you know.....?" That's how the conversation usually started outside the back doors in the 'smoking area'. Twice a day Millie and several coworkers took their 'smoke breaks' out on the back porch where they worked. **Twice a day Millie had the latest 'scoop'** about the supervisor, the 'big boss', and/or someone on the company's board of directors. She answered the company phones and ran the office 'in the front' where clients came in, so Millie had lots of 'scoops' to share - and she did.

Millie always had ideas about (a) what was wrong with the company, and (b) how she'd fix it. Problem was, she never shared her ideas or observations with anyone except the 'smoke break group'. No, Millie just liked to stir things up. She'd start stories (true or perhaps just her viewpoint) and then sit back and watch what happened.

Millie never imagined in her wildest dreams just what those effects could be, until one day she got 'the call' from the big boss's office.

"Millie, would you step into my office, please?" *What could the big boss possibly want with me?* Her mind raced as she walked down the hall toward the big corner office.

She raised her hand to knock, but **before her hand could even touch the door, it opened.** The look on the big boss's administrative assistant's face could have frozen hot coffee in an instant as she looked straight at Millie. She stepped around Millie on her way out of the office, leaving Millie facing Mr. Thompson across the smooth top of his big walnut desk. It was empty except for.....a digital recorder sitting right in front of him.

"Come on in, Millie. I want you to hear something." And he pressed 'play'. She couldn't believe her ears. *How could this be?* "How....? Where....?" It was all she could say as she heard her voice talking about how bad their company's client services were getting, how their deliveries were messed up, and how inept the boss was. **Funny how different it seemed now** that she was sitting across the desk from that same boss. Mr. Thompson stopped playing the recording for a minute.

"So Millie, why didn't you ever come to me or one of the supervisors with your concerns? Let's listen a bit more, shall we?" So they sat and listened to Millie talk **about who she'd "get rid of" and "how all these problems could be fixed"** for a few more minutes.

"You need to know that the smoking area sits right where our highest risk for break-ins is, so we have twenty-four hour video surveillance back there. **We've been trying to figure out where all the destructive rumors going around the company were coming from,** and I do believe we've found the answer. What do you think?

"Well, I was just talking, that's all. And it's true you know. We have been having trouble with our service and delivery times....." Millie's mind scrambled for an answer, excuses, anything!

"I was only trying to help, that's all, and...."
"HELP? You thought this destructive gossip, this talking about people behind their backs would....HELP? **Exactly how did you see that happening?"** Mr. Thompson's face was turning a dangerous shade of serious. This wasn't looking too good.

"Well, sir, I mean.....I guess maybe I could have....I mean I should have.....come to you....or at least to the person I was talking about....."

"Maybe? How about definitely, without a doubt, no other way will do, Millie? **You almost ruined several promising careers with your gossip and rumor spreading.** Thank goodness we found the source before we lost good people. As it is, we're going to lose one - you. We can't have this behavior." As she felt her world crumble, he continued.

"We work together here. We may disagree, and we may not always get our way, but we talk to each other up front, face to face. This behind the back stuff will ruin our company, and it'll ruin lives. When you leave this office, Millie, pack your personal items, turn in your keys and ID, and leave. You're fired. I hope you learn from this experience."

✳ ✳ ✳ ✳ ✳ ✳ ✳ ✳ ✳

"My friends, don't say cruel things about others! If you do, or if you condemn others, you are condemning God's Law. And if you condemn the Law, you put yourself above the Law and refuse to obey either it or God who gave it. God is our judge, and he can save or destroy us. What right do you have to condemn anyone?"

"If you can't say something nice, then don't say anything at all!" I can still hear one of my grandmother's friend's voices in the recesses of my memory. Thankfully, a mentor early in my working life gave me 'the rest of the story', as the famous radio talk show host Paul Harvey would say.

Here it is: **"If it's nice, say it wherever you please. If you can't say anything nice,** and you can't say it to the person's face, keep your mouth shut. God's the only one who needs to hear that kind of talk. And while you're telling God, pray for a heart-adjustment for yourself!"

As James so aptly puts it, what right DO we have to condemn anyone? None. None at all. We're here to be the Body of Christ - together. We're here to uphold one another, to uplift one another, and to work for God's glory and the Good News of Christ - together.

But you may say, **"It's so hard! It's much easier to talk ABOUT someone than it is to talk TO them!"** When that temptation strikes (and it will, if it hasn't yet), think of the often-used beginning to such destructive talk. It goes something like this: **"Haven't you heard? Well, with God as my witness....."**

How true that is! God surely IS a witness - our eternal, loving, grace-filled, God. And God certainly holds us accountable for the way we treat one another.

And that video surveillance camera? Picture it - in God's hands, in the hands of our judge, and our redeemer.

Haven't you heard?

Reflections

Why do you think people behave in ways similar to Millie?

If you were one of Millie's coworkers, and you discovered the source of destructive workplace rumors, what would you do? Why?

How do we handle the temptation to spread negative (or downright destructive) gossip?

Reflections (continued)

What is the right thing to do when someone shares such gossip with us?

How can positive, constructive gossip change an environment for the better?

14

Who's Gonna Know?

Look here, you rich people, weep and groan with anguish because of all the terrible troubles ahead of you. Your wealth is rotting away, and your fine clothes are moth-eaten rags. Your gold and silver have become worthless. The very wealth you were counting on will eat away your flesh in hell. **This treasure you have accumulated will stand as evidence against you on the day of judgment.**

For listen! Hear the cries of the field workers whom you have cheated of their pay. The wages you held back cry out against you. The cries of the reapers have reached the ears of the Lord Almighty.

You have spent your years on earth in luxury, satisfying your every whim. Now your hearts are nice and fat, ready for the slaughter. **You have condemned and killed good people who had no power to defend themselves against you.**

- James 5: 1-6 (New Living Translation)

And a final word to you arrogant rich: Take some lessons in lament. You'll need buckets for the tears when the crash comes upon you. Your money is corrupt and your fine clothes stink. Your greedy luxuries are a cancer in your gut, destroying your life from within. **You thought you were piling up wealth. What you've piled up is judgment.**

All the workers you've exploited and cheated cry out for judgment. The groans of the workers you used and abused are a roar in the ears of the Master Avenger. You've looted the earth and lived it up. But all you'll have to show for it is a fatter than usual corpse. **In fact, what you've done is condemn and murder perfectly good persons, who stand there and take it.**

- James 5: 1-6 (The Message Version)

* * * * * * * * *

Who's gonna know? The thought kept nagging at her mind as she picked up the phone to call the police. That woman and her three kids had just moved into the abandoned house next door. The place had been vacant for a few years now. At first she'd thought they'd bought the place, or at the very least rented it. In fact, **she'd become so used to ignoring the unkempt yard and vacant, staring windows** that it had taken her a few days to notice that the lawn was mowed and the patio swept.

Who's gonna know? Interesting though, that after a few days Lori noticed there were never any lights on in the house. The kids who lived there sure seemed to spend a lot of time at the house next door too. When she really began to watch, Lori noticed they always went over there in the mornings before school and at night before bedtime. So she'd taken a walk around the block to ask their neighbor. "Well," Janice had begun, somehow sensing that Lori's motive might not be too friendly, "You know they don't have any money. Those kids, well, it's pretty cold outside. We're all helping them. You don't need to worry. Who's gonna know?"

Who indeed? **Lori thought as she trudged back around the block.** The snow was beginning to fall now. Soon it would cover the ground. The house did look good. Lori had noticed the now-neat front yard as she'd stood on Janice's front porch. **The house had been for sale for three years.** Lori remembered Pete and Ann, the couple who used to live there. Sad how Pete had lost his job and Ann was diagnosed with breast cancer all in the same month. They'd finally sold the house to one of those "buy anything at rock-bottom" companies. Rumor was, those "investors" were snapping up all the houses they could and letting them run down on purpose. Then they could tear all the houses down and put in a mall or something.

Oh no! Lori looked down at her watch. *Yikes!* **It was past time to pick her son up at preschool.** As she dashed out the door, she decided **calling the cops would have to wait until later that afternoon.**

* * * * * * * * * *

"Mommy! Mommy! I got a gold star for my letters! Can we go to McDonalds? See, it's real big, and gold, and shiny, and everything! Can we?" Spencer bounced up and down so fast in front of Lori, it almost made her dizzy. She put a calming hand on his shoulder. "Slow down, buddy! Wow - that's one cool star you've got there. Sure, let's celebrate. McDonalds it is!"

"Welcome to McDonalds. What can I get you?" Lori looked up into a weary, but smiling face. "One kids' hamburger meal please, and......are you OK?" The worker seemed about to fall over as she caught herself on the counter. Lori read her name tag. **"Sue, are you OK?"**

"Oh, yes ma'am, I'm fine. **Just been working a lot, that's all.** Got three kids and no money. My man, well, he just up and left, so....here we are." Sue straightened up and smiled that weary smile again. "One Happy Meal and what for you, ma'am?"

Lori didn't recognize Sue, but Sue sure knew who Lori was. She was that back yard neighbor who kept spying on her and the kids, trying to see what they were up to. Janice, the nice neighbor, had warned Sue about Lori. Now here she was, right here. Janice had warned her. "If anybody'll report you living here, it'll be Lori. She lives right behind you." But what could she do? Sue almost had the money saved up to rent a place the right way. Almost. **She caught herself wishing Lori would get sick, or have an accident or something. Sue knew a lot about cars.** Maybe while Lori and her son were 'celebrating', she could sneak out and......*who's gonna know?* NO! The voice in her head was loud and clear, so clear that Sue froze in place for a second. Jamie, her oldest, had been to Sunday school with a friend last weekend. She'd come home, hugged Sue, and declared, **"I'm so glad we have love-treasure in our house, Mom! It's the best!"** Then she'd run next door to play with her new friends.

Just then, Sue heard a familiar voice. Janice! She turned around just in time to see Janice enter McDonalds with a whole troop of kids - six of them! *Oh my gosh! I know those kids. Those three are Janice's, and those three are.....*

"Hey Sue, how about some burgers all around? Your kids did great in school today!" Lori sank a little lower in the chair, but to her surprise, Spencer jumped out of his seat and raced over to the kids. "Guess what? I got a gold star too! Wanna sit with me?"

Lori got home over an hour later. That phone call to the police didn't seem so important now. A plan came together in her head. Love-treasure. So she picked up the phone to call her friend in real estate. "Hey Stan, can we get a place for a mom and her three kids? I want to pay for it for the year so she can get back on her feet, and I want to do it so she doesn't know who I am. Can we do that?"

Sue almost had a heart attack the next day when Stan stopped by her workplace. "A house? For us? Free?" Stan was loving this. "Yes ma'am. It's only two blocks from...from, well, from where you're staying now. Will that be OK? Oh, and all you'll have to pay is the water. Everything else is paid. Heat, electricity, phone, internet for the kids. OK?"

Lori sat in the back of the indoor playground. **Strange how she felt richer than she had in years.** *Who's gonna know?* She watched the joy and disbelief on Sue's face. Love-treasure. Now that was living!

✻ ✻ ✻ ✻ ✻ ✻ ✻ ✻ ✻

Many people read Scriptures like this one and immediately dismiss them. They think, *Not me!* They're not wealthy, so it must not apply to them. **Or they read Scriptures like this and use them to fuel a sort of "heavenly vengeance"** scenario. Maybe you've even found yourself in one of these two modes.

Here's the truth though: It's about focus. Is our focus on wanting, getting, and keeping "stuff"? Or do we see the material things as tools for spiritual growth and building of Christ-like community? Are we building ourselves up, or building up the Body of Christ?

This Scripture is for all of us. Think about it. **Each of us is richer in some worldly way than someone else.**

Who's gonna know?
God has known, does know, and will know.

Reflections

Think of a "next chapter" for this story. What do you think it might be?

How can you picture God continuing to work in each of these people's lives?

What would you have done in Lori's position?

15

Final Instructions

My friends, be patient until the Lord returns. Think of farmers who wait patiently for the spring and summer rains to make their valuable crops grow. Be patient like those farmers and don't give up. The Lord will soon be here! *Don't grumble about each other* or you will be judged, and the judge is right outside the door.

My friends, follow the example of the prophets who spoke for the Lord. They were patient, even when they had to suffer. In fact, we praise the ones who endured the most. You remember how patient Job was and how the Lord finally helped him because he is so merciful and kind.

My friends, above all else, don't take an oath. You must not swear by heaven or by earth or by anything else. "Yes" or "No" is all you need to say. If you say anything more, you will be condemned.

If you are having trouble, you should pray. And if you are feeling good, you should sing praises. If you are sick, ask the church's leaders to come and pray for you. Ask them to put olive oil on you in the name of the Lord. If you have faith when you pray for sick people, they will get well. The Lord will heal them, and if they have sinned, he will forgive them.

If you have sinned, you should tell each other what you have done. Then you can pray for one another and be healed. The prayer of an innocent person is powerful, and it can help a lot. Elijah was just as human as we are, and for three and a half years his prayer kept the rain from falling. But when he did pray for rain, it fell from the skies and made the crops grow.

My friends, if any followers have wandered away from the truth, you should try to lead them back. If you turn sinners from the wrong way, you will save them from death, and many of their sins will be forgiven.

- James 5: 7-20 (Contemporary English Version)

Meanwhile, friends, **wait patiently for the Master's arrival.....Stay steady and strong.**
...Friends, **don't complain about each other**...
...**Take the old prophets as your mentors**...What a gift life is for those who stay the course!...
...And **since you know that he cares, let your language show it**....
...**Are you hurting? Pray. Do you feel great? Sing**...
...Make this your common practice: Confess your sins to each other and pray for each other so that you can live together whole and healed...
...**My dear friends, if you know people who have wandered off from God's truth, don't write them off. Go after them**...

- James 5:7-20 (The Message, excerpted)

* * * * * * * * *

It was the final test - the Orienteering Challenge. Max needed to pass in order to get his instructor's certification so he could lead wilderness photography groups on weeklong trips. If he could just get through this last thing.....

THE CHALLENGE. Three days. Twenty-four compass-led stops to make in the wilderness of North Dakota - with 100% accuracy.

As Max pitched his tent, laid out his sleeping bag, and prepared his dinner, he knew the easy part was done. **One day down, two (the hardest) left.** Today had been perfect: great weather, easy going, and best of all, NO MISTAKES! Max hoped the next two days would go just as smoothly. Soon he relaxed and went to sleep with map and compass bearings swimming in his head.

Max woke up in the dark to a weird feeling. You know the kind that tells you something's not quite right? Yep - that one. He opened his eyes to find...the wall of his tent mere inches from his face. Whoa! As his mind quickly cleared, he realized the whole side of the small tent had caved in. But how...?

Wind! That was the eerie whining sound, and it meant just one thing in this terrain: fast-moving, strong storm! Max scrambled out into the dark, pressing the light-up button on the side of his watch: 2AM. Fighting against the strong wind, he yanked the tent stakes and bundled the tent up in one smooth, well-practiced move. Leaning into the cold wind and struggling to hang on to his gear, Max quickly lashed the gear together onto his backpack harness.

Compass and route map in easy reach in the pocket of his all-weather suit, **he headed off-course about two hundred yards to shelter between some boulders he'd spotted the evening before.** Just as he squeezed (glad he'd lost those twenty pounds!) into his narrow safe-haven, the first big fat drops of rain splatted against his refuge. Splat, splat, splat! Curled up tight with just barely enough space for himself and his gear, he waited out the storm. **Pouring rain and howling wind surrounded him**, the scene lit up every now and then by huge lightning bolts spreading across the sky.

3AM. 4AM. 5AM. As Max waited, tightly squeezed into a ball between those boulders , the muscles and joints of his six-foot-tall body cramped and twitched in pain.

6AM. The faint rays of sunrise lit the very edges of the small bit of eastern sky Max could see. Finally the rain settled down to a gentle pitter-patter, then stopped completely as the wind became a gentle breeze.

6:30AM. The sunrise painted the eastern sky as Max crawled out of his shelter feet first, pulling his gear behind him. Late! Just great.....

Now to retrace his course back, then pick up today's assigned route. Mud was everywhere! Slipping and sliding, leaning forward against the weight of his backpack, Max started out. **What was that weird noise? Was it a voice...out here?** There shouldn't be anyone within at least half a mile by now. Each of them had been given a unique course to run and none were designed to cross each other. But it sure sounded like a voice....

"Max! Hey, Max! Over here!" He looked a bit to the east, squinting his eyes against the now-bright sunshine and spotted what looked like a **walking, talking....mud-creature!** The voice sounded like his old buddy Walt, but how...?

"Hay Max!" Walt slid to a stop a few yards away. **"Hey buddy, I got lost last night.** I tried to correct my course, but then that wind started howling and all heck broke loose, you know? And well then....you can see what happened next. **Can you help me?"**

Max looked at Walt, then snuck a peek at his watch. **7AM. Great. Now he was an HOUR LATE** starting out. *Why me?* he thought as he shifted the weight of the harness and gear on his back.

"Well God ....." *Almost.* Max bit his tongue, remembering what his old mentor and teacher had taught him. Hmmm. What WOULD old Murphy say right now? Oh yeah, "No swearin', lots a' patience, plenty a' prayin', and help yer buddies." Max and Murph's other students had jokingly called it "Murph's Law". Yep, that was about it.

OK then. Murph's Law it was. "Walt, here's how it is then: there's a check point about midday on my test-route. I figure we'll get there about....one o'clock this afternoon - if we leave now and move fast. I'll lead you there and radio in for them to pick you up."

Walt thought a minute. **"But Max, you're GOOD. Can't you get me back on MY course?"**

7:15AM. Max bit his tongue again on another un-Murph-like word. "No, Walt, but I can, and will, lead you to safety. Now let's GO!!" And they went.

* * * * * * * * *

Final instructions. Like the words that rang in Max's mind as he faced hard times and decision making, James offered these last words of guidance to his readers. It's like this, "OK, I've given you the long version of how to live in Christ, now here's the summary!"

Max had to wait patiently. His plan? No, it's just what life seemed to dish out at the time.
What situations is life sending you right now, in which you need to hear "wait patiently for the Master"?

Max was indeed tempted to complain about Walt. Why didn't he pay more attention? How did he get lost anyway - wasn't he paying attention, or what?
How are we tempted to complain about one another?

Max remembered the words and guidance of his mentor Murphy.
What "prophets" and mentors has God placed in our lives to guide and help us?

Max had to "bite his tongue" against the temptation to use God's name in ways he shouldn't.
Are we careful to respect God as our Creator and Redeemer, the One who loves us dearly?

Max did complete the course, after guiding a still-grumbling Walt to that checkpoint. Over and over he was almost unbearably tempted to leave him behind. But again, Murph's words, his "final instructions" echoed through his mind and guided his actions: "No swearin', lots a' patience, plenty a' prayin', and help yer buddies."

As we "travel the course" of our lives, how do we treat others who have lost their way? Do we say to ourselves, "How sad for them." And to them, "Good luck, wish I could help you, but I'm..."? In other words, do we "write them off"? Listen again:

...My dear friends, if you know people who have wandered off from God's truth, don't write them off. Go after them...

And my friend, **if you are like Walt,** know that Jesus the Christ is earnestly seeking you. He's placing people in your life like Max, who will lead you to a "checkpoint" where you can reconnect with your Lord and Savior, Jesus. They may be those whom you least expect, and they may come to you in surprising ways, but they are there, and they will come. **Count on it - God will never abandon you. Ever.**

Reflections

Who do you identify with the most in this story? Why?

How is Max's Orienteering Challenge like your everyday life?

What does it feel like to know that God will never, ever abandon you?

First Peter

16

On Assignment

Peter, an apostle of Jesus Christ, To the exiles of the Dispersion in Pontus, Galatia, Cappadocia, Asia, and Bithynia, who have been chosen and destined by God the Father and sanctified by the Spirit to be obedient to Jesus Christ and to be sprinkled with his blood: May grace and peace be yours in abundance.

Blessed be the God and Father of our Lord Jesus Christ! **By his great mercy he has given us a new birth into a living hope through the resurrection of Jesus Christ** from the dead, and into an inheritance that is imperishable, undefiled, and unfading, kept in heaven for you, who are being protected by the power of God through faith for a salvation ready to be revealed in the last time.

In this you rejoice, even if now for a little while you have had to suffer various trials, so that the genuineness of your faith-- being more precious than gold that, though perishable, is tested by fire-- may be found to result in praise and glory and honor when Jesus Christ is revealed.   - 1 Peter 1: 1-7 (New Revised Standard Version)

I, Peter, am an apostle on assignment by Jesus, the Messiah, writing to exiles scattered to the four winds. Not one is missing, not one forgotten. God the Father has his eye on each of you, and has determined by the work of the Spirit to keep you obedient through the sacrifice of Jesus. May everything good from God be yours!

What a God we have! And how fortunate we are to have him, this Father of our Master Jesus! **Because Jesus was raised from the dead, we've been given a brand-new life** and have everything to live for, including a future in heaven - and the future starts now! God is keeping careful watch over us and the future. The day is coming when you'll have it all - life healed and whole.

I know how great this makes you feel, even though you have to put up with every kind of aggravation in the meantime. Pure gold put in the fire comes out <u>proved</u> pure; genuine faith put through this suffering comes out <u>proved</u> genuine. When Jesus wraps this all up, it's your faith, not your gold, that God will have on display as evidence of his victory.   - 1 Peter 1: 1-7 (The Message Version)

* * * * * * * * * *

"City Beat." Yeah, right. What they really mean is "Slum Beat", Micah thought to himself as he received his new assignment. "City Beat." What had he done to deserve this?

The only time he'd even seen these "City Beat" neighborhoods was out the windows of his Jaguar as he sped down the highway over the "depressed section" of the city. So now...now he was supposed to actually park and get out? Nope, not in his Jag. Micah had enough smarts to know that his shiny new yellow beauty wouldn't last five minutes down...there.

It was as if editor-in-chief Bob Simmons was reading his mind. He looked up from his desk. **"Oh, and Micah? Take the bus. Your ride, well, I'm sure you know how it would end up in City Beat territory.** Good luck, son. Filing deadline's four o'clock - sharp. Get a good story. I'm counting on you!"

The bus?

* * * * * * * * * *

On assignment - to the "exiles". That's the feeling that overwhelmed Micah that first day of his new territory as a writer for the city paper. **He'd had grand dreams:** press passes to football, basketball, baseball games (close, up-front seats - now we're talking!), meeting big important people, press parties........but THIS? Not even on his radar, nope, not at all!

"Scattered to the four winds..." That was exactly how it was - until Micah started meeting people - really meeting them - on his new "beat". Like the guy who'd moved back to his old neighborhood so he could make a difference with the kids, the restaurant server trying to keep the heat on in her tiny apartment for her three kids, and the cop who actually asked to work this neighborhood!

As weeks stretched into months, Micah's view changed. Instead of feeling like he was entering a foreign country each morning when he came to the "City Beat", he began to feel that way when he drove home. Punching the code into the alarmed gates at the entrance to his own neighborhood started to feel strange, like he was landing in an alien world. Now the problem wasn't so much finding a story to file by 4PM, but rather choosing between several stories, all worthy of printing and sharing with the world.

Micah spent very little time at his desk in the paper's offices any more. One day as he walked into the vast room that twenty reporters shared, **he spotted a note on his desk - on Bob Simpson's letterhead.** He quickly put his coat and laptop case down and opened the envelope. It said simply, **"Come see me."** Oh boy. What could this mean? Looking across the room to the clear glass that separated the reporters from the editor-in-chief's office, he realized that Bob Simpson was looking at him...and he was smiling (always a good sign). Micah walked across the room, dodging desks and people, and knocked on the boss's open door.

"Come on in, Micah. I have a new assignment for you!"
OK then, what now, maybe the city jail? Lost in his own (negative) thoughts, he almost missed his boss's next words.
"How does Amsterdam sound, Micah?"
Amster-what? "Sir? Did you just say...Amsterdam?"
Bob Simpson laughed, his eyes crinkling up and his infectious laugh carrying out into the newsroom. Several other reporters looked up, then looked quickly back down at their work.
"Yes, that's exactly what I said. Amsterdam. I figure you're pretty good at figuring out foreign cultures and filing some pretty amazing stuff, so how about it?"

Micah laughed to himself as he unpacked his gear in his new office - in downtown Amsterdam. He remembered his young niece asking him what he was going to do "way over there". "Oh, I'll be on assignment." As he pulled out the framed pictures he'd taken of the "City Beat" and hung them on his new walls, he remembered all the sights, smells, and sounds. The danger. The trials. The days he didn't think he could ride that bus one more day.

Now he was learning a new language, a new culture, and a new way of living. On assignment.

✳ ✳ ✳ ✳ ✳ ✳ ✳ ✳ ✳

You know, **Peter's experience isn't that much different from ours.** Each day is different: new people, new situations, new 'languages' to encounter. Every one of them prepares us for the next, and the next, and.....

Sometimes we're not too happy with where God places us 'on assignment'. I'm sure Peter had his unhappy days too, days of 'trials' and 'aggravation', days of learning and being refined by the power of the Holy Spirit.

Peter found immeasurable grace in his travels, even in the midst of trials and hard times. So did Micah. May it be that way for you and I.

Welcome to the Body of Christ: On Assignment!

Reflections

How is your everyday life like being in a foreign land, "on assignment"?

How do you react to the ending of this Scripture text?   What does it say to you?

"Pure gold put in the fire comes out <u>proved</u> *pure; genuine faith put through this suffering comes out* <u>proved</u> *genuine. When Jesus wraps this all up, it's your faith, not your gold, that God will have on display as evidence of his victory."*

17

Tug of...Grace

You love him even though you have never seen him. Though you do not see him, you trust him; and even now you are happy with a glorious, inexpressible joy. Your reward for trusting him will be the salvation of your souls.

This salvation was something the prophets wanted to know more about. They prophesied about this gracious salvation prepared for you, even though they had many questions as to what it all could mean. They wondered what the Spirit of Christ within them was talking about when he told them in advance about Christ's suffering and his great glory afterward. They wondered when and to whom all this would happen. They were told that these things would not happen during their lifetime, but many years later, during yours. And now this Good News has been announced by those who preached to you in the power of the Holy Spirit sent from heaven. It is all so wonderful that even the angels are eagerly watching these things happen.

So think clearly and exercise self-control. Look forward to the special blessings that will come to you at the return of Jesus Christ. *Obey God because you are his children. Don't slip back into your old ways of doing evil; you didn't know any better then.* **But now you must be holy in everything you do, just as God-- who chose you to be his children-- is holy.** *For he himself has said, "You must be holy because I am holy."*

- 1 Peter 1: 8-16 (New Living Translation)

You never saw him, yet you love him. You still don't see him, yet you trust him – with laughter and singing. Because you kept on believing, you'll get what you're looking forward to: total salvation.

The prophets who told us this was coming asked a lot of questions about this gift of life God was preparing. The Messiah's Spirit let them in on some of it – that the Messiah would experience suffering, followed by glory. They clamored to know who and when. All they were told was that they were serving you, you who by orders from heaven have now heard for yourselves – through the Holy Spirit – the Message of those prophesies fulfilled. Do you realize how fortunate you are? Angels would have given anything to be in on this!

So roll up your sleeves, put your mind in gear, be totally ready to receive the gift that's coming when Jesus arrives. *Don't lazily slip back into those old grooves of evil, doing just what you feel like doing. You didn't know any better then; you do now.* **As obedient children, let yourselves be pulled into a way of life shaped by God's life, a life energetic and blazing with holiness.** *God said, "I am holy; you be holy."*

- 1 Peter 1: 8-16 (The Message Version)

* * * * * * * * * *

"Oh boy! Tug of War! I LOVE Tug of War!"
"Me too! Let's do boys against girls!"
"Nah, too easy. Let's just draw for sides!"

Jim, the games leader, didn't even get a chance to talk! The kids saw the rope stretched out on the ground and the cones set up in the middle on the grass and took off. They were so excited!
"Whoa! Hey kids, hold up!" Jim jogged over to catch up with the young energy-loaded group. "So kids, what's this game all about?" He wanted to be sure they all started with the same rules for the Tug of War game.

Young Nick, quickly shaping up to be one of the leaders of the group, spoke right up. "Well, we get two teams – one on this side and one on that side. You say 'Go!' and we start pulling. The first team to pull the other one past those cones wins the war!"

Jim smiled. "OK then. Let's try that, but then **I have some other surprises in this box** for us to try after that." A couple of the kids tried to peek in the box Jim was holding, but he laughed and just held it tighter. "No deal! Let's play this first!" **Sally, another budding leader in the group, gave Jim 'the look' along with a big sigh and roll of her eyes.** "Man! Can't we just see real quick? Just a hint?" Jim lifted the box higher. "Nope. Time to play!"

So they drew numbers out of Jim's cap to form the teams. The rope was stretched out, teams took their places, and Jim yelled "Go!". Within seconds a winner was declared. After two more team-pickings and contests, Sally walked back over to Jim. "OK, what's in the box? Let's play a different game – this is BORING!"

"Everybody ready for a new game?" (lots of head nods)
"All right then. Sit on the grass and I'll show you this game I have in the box."
They all sat down, making sure they could see as Jim opened the box and began taking things out.
First came a big blob of blue…stuff. Next came an air pump. As he attached the pump to the blue blob and turned it on……..Oh, a big blue blow-up mat! Maybe it was a jumping game!

Wow! Was that mat ever BIG! A foot thick, it had to be a full five by ten feet! What was this game?
Jim moved the Tug of War cones out of the way, replacing them with the big mat. He placed a big towel over the middle of the mat. Nick thought he saw something written on that blue mat, but Jim covered it too fast for him to read it – rats!

Next he took two stacks of multi-colored cones out of the box, along with a stack of big labels. Hmmmm….
Jim re-stretched the rope out so its center passed right over the blue mat. Then he got to work with the new cones and labels.
"Hey, can you all help? How about if I give each of you a cone and a label. Can you stick the labels on the cones for me?" The kids were really eager now, anxious to see what this weird-looking game would be!

First he gave a blue cone and a label to Sally. "Worries", it said. Hmmmm.
Then Jim handed a yellow cone and a label that said, "Fear" to Aaron.
Soon labels and cones were everywhere! Labels like, "Mean people", "Sadness", "Hard jobs", "Sickness"….
What a lot of bad news! What WAS this game about, anyway?

Now the kids were confused – and REALLY curious!

"Bet you're wondering what this game's all about, aren't you? **Well, it works sort of like Tug of War, but I call it…..ready?   Tug of….GRACE!**" With that, Jim yanked the towel off the center of the big blue mat so they could all read the big white letters on the mat: "GRACE".

"All right. Let's pick teams like we did before and I'll show you how to play. Once again they picked numbers out of Jim's cap and separated into two teams.

"Well kids, the goal of this game is a bit different," Jim told them as he scattered the labeled cones around the rope, half on each side of the ends of the stretched-out rope. "Instead of pulling the other team over the middle line to win, the idea is to pull them past all this stuff on the cones and onto the big soft mat of grace in the middle."

Sally was catching on, but her competitive streak was coming out too. **"Wait a minute. So we're trying to pull the other team to the middle so THEY can win?** I mean, really, when you get to grace, you win, right?"

Not to be outdone, Nick joined in. **"So winning is losing, and losing is winning, right? This is confusing! If we pull them into the 'Grace Pit' – cool name, huh? – they're looking good, but us, well we're stuck out in the middle of all this! How is that good?"**

Jim smiled. These kids were GOOD! "Well, let's see if we can work that out. Maybe there's a way we can all get to the 'Grace Pit' – great name, Nick – together…."

So they lined up, half on each end of the rope, labeled cones scattered around, and the "Grace Pit" in the middle. **The game didn't start nearly as fast this time.** The rules had changed!

But soon one team was pulling away and the other ended up in the big soft "Grace Pit". The team in the middle almost dropped the rope out of habit, but then all of a sudden one of them yelled, **"Quick, pull them in too!"** and the Grace Pit was energized. Within minutes the Grace Pit was a mass of giggling, bouncing kids having a great time.

Then Nick and one of his new buddies noticed Jim standing outside the Grace Pit. "Get Him!" he yelled. Four kids jumped out of the Grace Pit, chased Jim down, and dragged him back to the Grace Pit! "Can't leave anyone out of grace, right Jim?" Nick said, a twinkle in his eye.

So it was that "Grace Pit" became the all-time favorite game at summer camp!

✳ ✳ ✳ ✳ ✳ ✳ ✳ ✳ ✳

"When you get to grace, you win, right?" How true that is!

"As obedient children, let yourselves be pulled into a way of life shaped by God's life, a life energetic and blazing with holiness."

Those kids had it right. Life is a big "tugging" game in many ways, isn't it? "Winning" in the worldly sense isn't always real winning, is it?

When they saw Jim outside the "Grace Pit", they sent a team to go out and bring him in.

What an example that is for the rest of us! How can we spend more of our lives in God's grace, allowing Him to pull and shape us with the Spirit's energy and blazing holiness? Couldn't we help others find and experience God's amazing "tug of grace" too?

Reflections

Thinking about life in general, what do you think the difference is between "tug of war" and "tug of grace"?

When Nick says, "So winning is losing and losing is winning.", what do you think he means?

How can we be open to letting ourselves "be pulled into a way of life shaped by God's life, a life energetic and blazing with holiness"?

18

Ring in the New...Life!

If you invoke as Father the one who judges all people impartially according to their deeds, live in reverent fear during the time of your exile. **You know that you were ransomed from the futile ways inherited from your ancestors, not with perishable things like silver or gold, but with the precious blood of Christ,** *like that of a lamb without defect or blemish. He was destined before the foundation of the world, but was revealed at the end of the ages for your sake.*

Through him you have come to trust in God, who raised him from the dead and gave him glory, so that your faith and hope are set on God. Now that you have purified your souls by your obedience to the truth so that you have genuine mutual love, love one another deeply from the heart.

You have been born anew, not of perishable but of imperishable seed, through the living and enduring word of God. *For "All flesh is like grass and all its glory like the flower of grass. The grass withers, and the flower falls, but the word of the Lord endures forever." That word is the good news that was announced to you.*

- 1 Peter 1: 17-25 (New Revised Standard Version)

You say that God is your Father, but God doesn't have favorites! He judges all people by what they do. So you must honor God while you live as strangers here on the earth. **You were rescued from the useless way of life that you learned from your ancestors. But you know that you were not rescued by such things as silver or gold that don't last forever. You were rescued by the precious blood of Christ,** *that spotless and innocent lamb. Christ was chosen even before the world was created, but because of you, he did not come until these last days.*

And when he did come, it was to lead you to have faith in God, who raised him from death and honored him in a glorious way. That's why you have put your faith and hope in God. You obeyed the truth, and your souls were made pure. Now you sincerely love each other.

But you must keep on loving with all your heart. Do this because **God has given you new birth by his message that lives on forever.** *The Scriptures say, "Humans wither like grass, and their glory fades like wild flowers. Grass dries up, and flowers fall to the ground. But what the Lord has said will stand forever." Our good news to you is what the Lord has said.*

- 1 Peter 1: 17-25 (Contemporary English Version)

* * * * * * * * *

"Well Joe, I'm sure glad the new year is over. Man, what a mess!" Ned's forehead glistened with sweat as he kept mopping the big social hall. Joe looked up as he hauled yet another load of trash through to the back doors. **"Over? Nah, it's just beginning. We've got three hundred sixty-three more days to go!"**

Ned stopped to pull a bandana from his back pocket to catch the sweat which was now dripping down his nose. **"Oh no we don't! I'm not having another three hundred sixty-three of these!** Want to know what my wife said yesterday? She said it's time we started living like it really was a new year. You know I dropped out of school, but I was just a kid then. **It's time to really ring in a new year. No, wait, I've got it - I'm ringing in a new LIFE!** Tomorrow I'm starting classes that will get me ready to take the GED. And I'm going to pass that thing too, because after that comes architecture college. I figure I've sure cleaned enough of these - now it's my turn to design a few!"

Joe couldn't believe that change that came over Ned as he talked. **The old Ned seemed to disappear right in front of him.** The 'resigned to my fate' look transformed into a 'look out, new things are coming' face, all within the minutes they'd been talking! **"Ring in a new life, huh? Well, maybe at your age,** but I'm pushing fifty, and...." He ran a hand over the top of his head, smoothing the few hairs he had left up there. His barber had told him just last week to give up on the comb-over thing and just enjoy his 'perfect head'. Yeah, right, uh huh. Joe was so lost in his own thoughts that he only looked up when Ned cleared his throat.

"Fifty? Man, you'd better be checking in at the old folks home, right? I mean buddy, you're one foot in the grave. Is that what I'm hearing? Because if it is, you need to get a reality check. Man! You've got decades ahead of you - decades! **Who says you can't do just what my Trudy told me to do - ring in a new life! Why not?"**

"Well Ned, if we're talking about dreams, well, you know I raised five boys by myself, don't you? Well, my dream's to start a program kind of like Big Brothers - only for single dads. Maybe a 'Dad's Big Brother' sort of thing, you know, to mentor those dads. God knows I could have used a 'big brother' to stand by me all those years!"

"Now you're talking! That's exactly what you've been for me these last couple of years. When my girlfriend Mandy left baby Joshua on my doorstep, I didn't know the first thing about kids, let alone babies! Remember that?" Joe chuckled. Boy did he remember! Ned looked him straight in the eye. "I don't think we would have made it without you - really, Joe."

"Hey, and we've got men's group at church tonight too. **You ever think about asking Pastor Rick** about your idea? He was **just preaching about letting Jesus have a new year every year of our lives.** Maybe he's ready to put that preachin' to work!"

That was how the Man 2 Man single dads network began. After six years, the program had grown so much that the church began looking for new space to house its many ministries. Guess what Ned's first architectural design project was? You got it - they called it the **"Man Up Club" - men giving other men a hand up and a shoulder to lean on.** Ned and Joe truly rang in a new life that year - and every year after that!

* * * * * * * * *

How about us? **When New Year's Day rolls around each year, is it 'over' on January 2nd?**
Do you live each day, each year, as if God has truly "...given you new birth by his message that lives on forever..."? Don't just "ring in the new year", ring in a new life each and every day!

God didn't send Jesus for only one day, or even just one year. He sent Jesus for each and every one of us - for each and every day of our lives! How are you 'ringing in the new life' God has given you in Christ through grace today?

It's not too late to start - how about it?

Reflections

Why do people get to the point where they think "it's too late"?

What would it look like for you to "ring in a new life"?

What does New Year's Day mean to you? Perhaps it means a lot. Do you gather with friends and/or family to share a special time? Maybe you hardly notice it. Is it just another day for you? Why do you think this is? If it's not anything different, are there other days which are "new year" times for you?

What would you say to Joe?

19

Trash to Treasure

So get rid of all malicious behavior and deceit. Don't just pretend to be good! Be done with hypocrisy and jealousy and backstabbing. **You must crave pure spiritual milk so that you can grow into the fullness of your salvation.** *Cry out for this nourishment as a baby cries for milk, now that you have had a taste of the Lord's kindness.* **Come to Christ, who is the living cornerstone of God's temple. He was rejected by the people, but he is precious to God who chose him.**

And now God is building you, as living stones, into his spiritual temple. *What's more, you are God's holy priests, who offer the spiritual sacrifices that please him because of Jesus Christ. As the Scriptures express it, "I am placing a stone in Jerusalem, a chosen cornerstone, and anyone who believes in him will never be disappointed." Yes, he is very precious to you who believe."*

"But for those who reject him, "The stone that was rejected by the builders has now become the cornerstone." And the Scriptures also say, "He is the stone that makes people stumble, the rock that will make them fall." They stumble because they do not listen to God's word or obey it, and so they meet the fate that has been planned for them.

But you are not like that, for **you are a chosen people.** *You are a kingdom of priests, God's holy nation, his very own possession.* **This is so you can show others the goodness of God, for he called you out of the darkness into his wonderful light.** *Once you were not a people; now you are the people of God. Once you received none of God's mercy; now you have received his mercy."*

- 1 Peter 2: 1-10 (New Living Translation)

So clean house! *Make a clean sweep of malice and pretense, envy and hurtful talk. You've had a taste of God. Now, like infants at the breast,* **drink deep of God's pure kindness. Then you'll grow up mature and whole in God.**

Welcome to the living Stone, the source of life. *The workmen took one look and threw it out; God set it in the place of honor.* **Present yourselves as building stones for the construction of a sanctuary vibrant with life,** *in which you'll serve as holy priests offering Christ-approved lives up to God. The Scriptures provide precedent: "Look! I'm setting a stone in Zion, a cornerstone in the place of honor. Whoever trusts in this stone as a foundation will never have cause to regret it."*

To you who trust him, he's a Stone to be proud of, but to those who refuse to trust him, "The stone the workmen threw out is now the chief foundation stone." For the untrusting it's "...a stone to trip over, a boulder blocking the way." They trip and fall because they refuse to obey, just as predicted.

But you are the ones chosen by God, *chosen for the high calling of priestly work, chosen to be a holy people,* **God's instruments to do his work and speak out for him, to tell others of the night-and-day difference he made for you - from nothing to something, from rejected to accepted.** - 1 Peter 2: 1-10 (The Message Version)

* * * * * * * * * *

The old book sat in a forgotten corner of the closet: on the top shelf (the kind you need a chair to get to), in the back corner. You know, the place you put things you've either long-ago forgotten and/or only pay attention to when you're moving?

Amy growled to herself in frustration as she hauled the stepstool into the bedroom closet. Thumping it down on the floor, she climbed up to get those last things from the back corner of that top shelf. She ran her hand along the shelf, raking out clumps of dust and chunks of cobweb debris onto her head. Yuk!! After two unsuccessful grabs, Amy finally got hold of the corner of the old book and pulled it out. *Why was she keeping this?*

In the last few months, **everything that could go wrong in her life had seemed to do just that.** The cancer that killed her mom, just a year after losing her dad. Losing her job and scholarship when she chose to help care for her mom. Now just yesterday, her fiance' handed her another surprise: he'd found 'someone else'. Great, just great.
No job meant no money. No money meant no apartment. And no apartment meant moving back home to her parents' old house to basically start over.

Old book in hand, Amy almost forgot she was on the <u>second</u> step of the stool. *Perfect, all I need is a broken leg!* Still grumbling, she tossed the old book in the last box.

Later that day as she unloaded the rental truck at her folks' old house, Amy was surprised when her Great Uncle Benny's car pulled up in the driveway. She ran out to hug him and soon found herself crying, sobbing really, on his soft shoulder, wrapped in his frail (but determined) embrace.

Uncle Benny kept her company as she unloaded and unpacked, telling old family stories one after the other. Soon she was down to that last box - the one from her bedroom closet. Suddenly Uncle Benny, busily chatting on about the 'old days', stopped mid-sentence. That <u>never</u> happened! **Amy's hand froze halfway out of the box, that old dusty book ready to be tossed into the trash.**

He slowly reached out his hand toward the book. **"Is that....?" His voice shook. "It couldn't be! Amy, do you know what you've got?"** He gently took it from her hand, tears welling in his eyes. "Where did you get this?"

"Umm.....the back of my closet? I think I got it in a box of old stuff when grandmother died. **I don't know why I never threw it out before...I mean, I can't even read it!"**

"Amy, you've been grumbling all day, feeling sorry for yourself, talking about having to start your life all over again, right?" She nodded, seeing the serious look of purpose in his eyes. **"Can I read some of this to you?"** Again she nodded and sat down beside him on the bed.

He wiped a tear from the corner of his eye as he began. **"The title says, 'From Nothing to Hope'."** Uncle Benny ran his finger over the Japanese characters on the cover. Then he opened the book very carefully. The binding gave out soft crackling protests as he turned the first page. In a voice that matched the crackling pages, he began to read.

"Day One. We have nothing left. They've brought us to this camp place. Father says to pretend we're woods-camping like we used to do, but we have nothing! We left our house, our garden, my books and toys. How long will they make us stay here? The worker guards here are so mean. They seem afraid of us. Why?" Uncle paused, wiping another tear away. He turned a few pages.

"**Day Five. I get it. We're never going home.** I think we'll die here. They hate us. They call us names. Why can't we go back home? Why?"

Amy interrupted. "**What's she talking about, Uncle?**" He smiled and brushed a hand across his eyes again. "**Ever heard of the Internment Camps, Amy?**" She nodded. "Wasn't that what they did to the Japanese people in World War Two?" Uncle Benny shook his head, sadness reflected in his eyes.

"**Amy, you are Japanese American. So was your grandmother - my sister. She wrote this.**" His ninety-plus year old hand caressed the page, then Amy's cheek. "Your grandmother, she wrote this book to speak hope into the lives of anyone who thought they'd lost it all, who thought they had to start all over...like you, Amy."

That day Amy learned what it was to really move "From Nothing to Hope". Grandmother told many of what she called "Trash to Treasure" stories in her book. Uncle Benny found the shortest and the longest entries in Grandmother's diary-book and read them last.

"**Day 143. Met Jesus. Found Hope.**"

"**Day 144. Got baptized today.** Water cold. What a day!....(half a page describing the wonder of that day)..... **Now I have a foundation for my hope.** My new life begins today. I am one of God's holy instruments playing in Jesus' band. I can see the light now. **I am not trash. I am treasure!**"

Uncle Benny turned to Amy. "**And you, young lady, you are treasure too.** I will translate this all for you. You will need it, I think. Let your grandmother speak to you of temporary trash...and forever treasure. Let her walk with you in your new beginnings."

* * * * * * * * * *

"*So clean house! .... drink deep of God's pure kindness. Then you'll grow up mature and whole in God. Welcome to the living Stone, the source of life.* The workmen took one look and threw it out; God set it in the place of honor. *Present yourselves as building stones for the construction of a sanctuary vibrant with life, ...* Whoever trusts in this stone as a foundation will never have cause to regret it."

"**But you are the ones chosen by God,** chosen for the high calling of priestly work, chosen to be a holy people, **God's instruments to do his work and speak out for him,** to tell others of the night-and-day difference he made for you - from nothing to something, from rejected to accepted."

In many ways, we are just like Amy, just like her grandmother. We need to hear these words, no, not just hear them, but write them on our hearts as the prophet Jeremiah tells us. (Jeremiah 31:31-33)

Have you written these words on your heart?
How do they affect your daily life? How do you see yourself - as God's treasure?

Many times, **the world will tell you that you are more like trash than treasure.** Amy's world did that. Her grandmother's world certainly did. Ours does too.

Let God work, writing a new story, a new identity on your heart. I guarantee you that you will see more and more 'treasure' in your self as you let grace soak your heart and your life!

Reflections

What was the biggest surprise or 'aha' moment of this story for you?

Jeremiah 31:31-33 says this: "Jeremiah 31:31-34
"The day is coming," says the Lord, "when I will make a new covenant with the people of Israel and Judah. This covenant will not be like the one I made with their ancestors when I took them by the hand and brought them out of the land of Egypt. They broke that covenant, though I loved them as a husband loves his wife," says the Lord. "But this is the new covenant I will make with the people of Israel on that day," says the Lord. "I will put my instructions deep within them, and I will write them on their hearts. I will be their God, and they will be my people. And they will not need to teach their neighbors, nor will they need to teach their relatives, saying, 'You should know the Lord.' For everyone, from the least to the greatest, will know me already," says the Lord. "And I will forgive their wickedness, and I will never again remember their sins." (New Living Translation)

What does this mean to you?

What would it mean in your life for God to turn your "trash" to "treasure"?

20

Temporary Quarters

Beloved, I urge you as aliens and exiles to abstain from the desires of the flesh that wage war against the soul. **Conduct yourselves honorably among the Gentiles,** *so that, though they malign you as evildoers,* **they may see your honorable deeds and glorify God** *when he comes to judge.*

For the Lord's sake accept the authority of every human institution, whether of the emperor as supreme, or of governors, as sent by him to punish those who do wrong and to praise those who do right. For it is God's will that by doing right you should silence the ignorance of the foolish.

As servants of God, live as free people, yet do not use your freedom as a pretext for evil. Honor everyone. Love the family of believers. Fear God. *Honor the emperor.*

- 1 Peter 2: 11-17 (New Revised Standard Version)

Dear friends, you are foreigners and strangers on this earth. So I beg you not to surrender to those desires that fight against you. *Always let others see you behaving properly, even though they may still accuse you of doing wrong. Then on the day of judgment, they will honor God by telling the good things they saw you do.*

The Lord wants you to obey all human authorities, especially the emperor, who rules over everyone. You must also obey governors, because they are sent by the emperor to punish criminals and to praise good citizens. God wants you to silence stupid and ignorant people by doing right. **You are free, but you are God's servants, and you must not use your freedom as an excuse for doing wrong. Respect everyone and show special love for God's people.** *Honor God and respect the emperor.*

- 1 Peter 2: 11-17 (Contemporary English Version)

* * * * * * * * * *

Basic training. These words evoke interesting feelings and some even more interesting responses. Ever feel like you stepped into an **alien world?** Well, the experience of military Basic Training definitely qualifies. Ever feel like you're not only behind the 'learning curve', but it just plain left the station without you? Again, the Basic training experience qualifies.

First, you lose your name. No matter who you've been all your life so far, now you become "soldier" (or "airman", or...). Oh, and your new favorite color is (drum roll, please)...army green and/or khaki. Good thing I liked those colors to begin with.

Second, you learn the true meaning of the saying, "hurry up and wait". Yeah, right. Oops, I really meant "Yes Sir/Ma'am!".

Oh, don't get me wrong, **the recruiters tell you about Basic - well, sort of.** "It's only eight weeks." "You'll get in terrific shape!" Yeah, stuff like that. Those things are true - and a whole lot more. It is only eight weeks, you will get in shape, both physically (although smart people work on that before Basic) and mentally. You will learn teamwork, organization, and discipline - all very useful and necessary skills to develop, especially in today's fast-paced world.

But, as with all new experiences, **there definitely are surprises!** My first surprise came as I boarded the bus taking me to Basic. **"Welcome, soldiers! Look around! These are your first temporary quarters!"** *OK, this is a weird greeting.* I thought a whole lot of things, but belonging to ROTC in high school made me smart enough not to say any of them. Not so for the young man in the seat in front of me.

"What?", he asked. All eyes were now fastened securely on the scene in front of the bus. "You say something, soldier?" Oh, yes, that voice could be heard, loud and clear. Ever seen a whole group cringe? Well, we did. Not to be deterred, the young man continued. **"Sir, well, I just wondered, what are 'temporary quarters'?"**

Well, anyone who was breathing at this point was doing so out of necessity, and as quietly as possible. "Sarge" was now mere inches from the young questioner, but his volume was no less. Then an interesting thing happened. **Sarge smiled.** *Not good,* I thought, *not good at all.* **His voice took on a sugary, slippery tone.** *Really not good.* "Well, soldier, it means don't get used to it. In fact, get used to not getting used to it - get it? You have no permanent quarters. None. It's all temporary." Sarge backed up, raised his head - and his voice - and addressed all of us. **"Listen up! The only permanent quarters you've got are these: Respect. Honor. Diligence. Got it? Everything else is temporary.** Got it? Let me hear it!" We were fast learners. A whole bus load of new 'soldiers' responded as one: "Yes SIR!" *Whew!*

Sarge sat down. The bus began its journey. To new 'temporary quarters'.

* * * * * * * * *

How many of us truly see our current situation, our current home, job, etc. as 'temporary quarters'? One common saying among those who do view earthly life this way is, "You can't take it with you!" Probably not many people actually live this way; however, we can see examples around us of those who do.

Perhaps you know someone who lives life to 'get the most bang for the buck', who doesn't really think about other people. These people are mostly concerned for themselves - mostly, because very few of us lives 100% one way or another. They are the **'here and now' folks.**

Then there are people who live in these 'temporary quarters' in a completely different way. What matters to them is exactly the opposite of those I just mentioned. These folks place life priorities on the eternal. They ask such questions as these: How does what I'm doing (or thinking of doing) affect other people, my community, my relationship with God? What does it say and show about my walk with Jesus as His follower? **These are the 'eternally aware' folks.**

So where does that leave most of us? In the middle. That's right. **Some days** we're more like those 'here and now' worldly citizens. After all, it's a crazy world, right? Got to survive, right? **Other days,** we're more like the 'eternally aware' folks. Sometimes it's out of desperation. You know the times. We ask God things like, 'Is this all there is, God?' or, 'How long, God?' or......... Sometimes we look around and wonder. We see the vastness of the universe - at least the small part we can comprehend - and we marvel. "Wow, God, how amazing! I'm so glad this isn't all there is!", we exclaim. We catch a glimpse in those moments of the eternal.

Jesus the Christ knows. He lived as man and God in one. Peter is counseling us to keep our eyes on the eternal. Christ kept his eyes on God - always. We should too. Peter reminds us that we who follow Christ as Lord and Savior claim an eternal inheritance. This means that **we are truly foreigners, strangers, exiles, aliens - whatever word best describes the situation for you - on this earth. Our eternal home is with Christ!**

Does this mean we can do whatever we want here? Not at all! We are to be recognizable as citizens of heaven. If I go to, China, let's say, and claim to be from the United States but know no English and nothing about life in the U.S., will the Chinese who meet me believe it? Not at all! Likewise for us who claim to be Christ-followers. **Are we recognizable?** Do we speak and act more and more each day with the language and behavior of our Master? If so, we are truly citizens of heaven! If not, well, we have some life-decisions to make, right?

As we live, work, and dream in these 'temporary quarters', let's keep our eyes on the eternal, permanent quarters God has prepared for us through the gift of his Son!

Reflections

So, how are we recognizable? Do we speak and act more and more each day with the language and behavior of our Master?

How do you deal with the "here and now" people in your life?

Do you know anyone who is more like an "eternally aware" person? How does being with them make you feel?

What are some good ways to, as Peter counsels, keep our eyes on the eternal while living daily in the world?

21

Silent Grace

You who are slaves must accept the authority of your masters. Do whatever they tell you-- not only if they are kind and reasonable, but even if they are harsh. For God is pleased with you when, for the sake of your conscience, you patiently endure unfair treatment.

Of course, you get no credit for being patient if you are beaten for doing wrong. But if you suffer for doing right and are patient beneath the blows, God is pleased with you. This suffering is all part of what God has called you to. **Christ, who suffered for you, is your example. Follow in his steps.**

He never sinned, and he never deceived anyone. He did not retaliate when he was insulted. When he suffered, he did not threaten to get even. **He left his case in the hands of God, who always judges fairly.**

He personally carried away our sins in his own body on the cross so we can be dead to sin and live for what is right. You have been healed by his wounds! **Once you were wandering like lost sheep. But now you have turned to your Shepherd, the Guardian of your souls.**

- 1 Peter 2: 18-25 (New Living Translation)

You who are servants, be good servants to your masters - not just to good masters, but also to bad ones. What counts is that you put up with it for God's sake when you're treated badly for no good reason. There's no particular virtue in accepting punishment that you well deserve. But if you're treated badly for good behavior and continue in spite of it to be a good servant, that is what counts with God.

This is the kind of life you've been invited into, the kind of life Christ lived. He suffered everything that came his way **so you would know that it could be done, and also how to do it, step-by-step.**

He never did one thing wrong, not once said anything amiss.

They called him every name in the book and he said nothing back. He suffered in silence, content to let God set things right. He used his servant body to carry our sins to the Cross so we could be rid of sin, free to live the right way. His wounds became your healing. You **were lost sheep with no idea who you were or where you were going.** Now **you're named and kept for good by the Shepherd of your souls.** *- 1 Peter 2: 18-25 (The Message Version)*

* * * * * * * * *

It was a unique invitation. "Servants' Party" was all it said on the front. The inside was just as plain. The date, time, and location was listed, along with these words: **"Servants only. No others. Invitation required for admittance."** Our church received ten such invitations with an accompanying letter instructing the pastor

70

to give them to "ten servants for Christ". What? The pastor brought the package to the outer office and handed it to the administrative assistant. "Here, Becky. This is right up your alley. Would you pass these out?"

Becky turned to those of us who just happened to be in the office. **"OK, so who wants one of THESE?"** Jeff, the church maintenance guy, picked up the empty package. "Wonder who sent them? Where's this party being held?"

Becky read one of the invitations. **"Ah, now I get it. It's those college students again.** It's at the chapel on campus, in the social hall. That explains it. They do crazy things like this every now and then. I bet they sent invitations to every church in town. **Wonder how many will actually go?"**

Jeff got serious. "Becky, you should go. If anyone around here qualifies as a servant, it's you." Becky laughed. "If you only knew, Jeff. If you only knew what I'm thinking sometimes, what I say to myself in that closet over there..."

Jeff wasn't giving up. "I'm not talking about any of that, and I think you know it. I've known you for at least five years now, and I say you should go."

Becky got that 'I've got a great idea and we're in it together' look that we all knew so well. *Uh oh, here it comes.....* She grinned. "We're ALL going! Strength in numbers, right? We'll be the best, strongest servant team there! Friday night, 6PM. We'll meet here and carpool. Right?" The other thing you need to know is that nobody, I mean NOBODY could easily say no to Becky - mostly because we all looked up to her as such a great example of... servanthood!

So we met in the church parking lot at 6PM sharp. Not so surprisingly, Becky had a total of ten people there! **That servants' party WAS unique.** It truly was 'invitation only'. The invitations were collected at the door as we signed in. Then we were invited to be seated. Instructions were given for the evening, and those who changed their minds were invited to do just that - change their minds and leave. Some did.

The instructions went something like this: **"This evening is an exercise in the experience of servanthood.** You may do nothing for yourself from now until nine o'clock this evening (except use the restroom). We'll gather in the chapel for worship and to pray for each other then."

OK. **This was a dinner party. We were all hungry. But....we could do nothing for ourselves!** Not hanging up our own coats. Not getting our own food, not even feeding ourselves! Not even wiping our own faces! We were partnered with someone we didn't know before that evening. We laughed together. We got frustrated. We learned. A lot. **That nine o'clock worship was one of the most powerful worship experiences I've ever had.** It was almost totally silent. For thirty minutes, we were to silently pray for our servant-partner. Then we came to the Communion Table and served one another, leaving in silence.

* * * * * * * * *

Was there more than laughter at the Servants' Party? Oh yeah. Mistakes were made, spills happened. One physical altercation was narrowly missed when an iced drink went down the front of - well, you get the picture. **Being a servant wasn't (and isn't) all 'sweetness and light'.** That was one of the points of the evening, and it was well made.

In many ways, we live in situations much like those of the Servants' Party. When we really think about it, we are dependent on each other for quite a bit. We depend on God for so much more - in fact, for everything. But we tend to be a noisy people - correction, a noisy, wandering-sheep kind of people. How content are we (really) to follow in the footsteps of our eternal Shepherd?

How do we react to the everyday 'unfairness' of the world we live in?
Is our reaction one that Jesus would recognize as part of holy servanthood? As Peter says, *"Now you're named and kept for good by the Shepherd of your souls."* Is this true?
Does it demonstrate our dependence on God as the judge? Do we really live as if, *He left his case in the hands of God, who always judges fairly."*?

No, we're not perfect. Far from it! Jesus the Christ was, and is, perfect. We're the sheep; He's the Shepherd. We're grace-learners; He's grace-full. May we keep learning, and living, in His eternal grace.

Reflections

Picture yourself at the "Servants' Party". What would your reactions be? Think all the way from receiving the invitation to experiencing the worship at the end.

What does the term "silent grace" mean to you? Can you think of any examples from your own life?

22

Holy Advantage

*Wives, in the same way, accept the authority of your husbands, so that, even if some of them do not obey the word, they may be won over without a word by their wives' conduct, when they see the purity and reverence of your lives. Do not adorn yourselves outwardly by braiding your hair, and by wearing gold ornaments or fine clothing; rather, **let your adornment be the inner self with the lasting beauty** of a gentle and quiet spirit, which is very precious in God's sight.*

It was in this way long ago that the holy women who hoped in God used to adorn themselves by accepting the authority of their husbands. Thus Sarah obeyed Abraham and called him lord. You have become her daughters as long as you do what is good and never let fears alarm you.

Husbands, in the same way, show consideration for your wives in your life together, paying honor to the woman as the weaker sex, since they too are also heirs of the gracious gift of life-- so that nothing may hinder your prayers.   -

1 Peter 3: 1-7 (New Revised Standard Version)

*The same goes for you wives: Be good wives to your husbands, responsive to their needs. There are husbands, who, indifferent as they are to any words about God, will by captivated by your holy beauty. **What matters is not your outer appearance - the styling of your hair, the jewelry you wear, the cut of your clothes - but your inner disposition.***

Cultivate inner beauty, the gentle, gracious kind that God delights in. The holy women of old were beautiful before God that way, and were good, loyal wives to their husbands. Sarah, for instance, taking care of Abraham, would address him as "my dear husband". You'll be true daughters of Sarah if you do the same, unanxious and unintimidated.

*The same goes for you husbands. Be good husbands to your wives. Honor them; delight in them. **As women they lack some of your advantages. But in the new life of God's grace, you're equals. Treat your wives, then, as equals so your prayers don't run aground.*** *- 1 Peter 3: 1-7 (The Message Version)*

* * * * * * * * * *

"You want him to notice you, right?" The young ladies were sitting at a table across the aisle from me, sipping their drinks. Jeans, hoodies and backpacks identified them as probable students from the local high school. Intrigued, I munched on my salad and listened.

One of them offered a suggestion. "Well, you've got to look right. Fix your hair up, girl!"
"Yeah," another added, **"Get a scoop neck and some of those smooth jeans too. You've got it; show it!"**

I glanced quickly over at the table. The young woman receiving the advice looked attractive just as she was. Hmmm....

"You know my mom would never let me wear something like that. I'd have to sneak it out of the house and change at school." Her face showed discomfort at this idea.

"Oh Molly, come on! **You want him to notice you or not?** You want a date for prom....or not?"

The other young lady chimed in. "All guys notice is, you know, well, just get some different clothes, that's all. I even have some you could borrow. We're the same size..." The first friend leaned across the table toward Molly. "Girlfriend, get real! **You need an advantage. You look good; let him see it!"**

"Thanks, but **I think I already have an advantage. I am real.** I have a brain, and I have personality. If I show him everything, what's left to wonder about? What's left to figure out? If I was him, I've already got, well, most anyway of what I want, so why go out? I'd want a real girlfriend, not a fake."

"Hey, no problem. We're just trying to help you get all the advantage you can."

"Well, thanks, I know you're just trying to help, but I want a different kind of advantage."
A look of 'aha!' crossed her friend Julie's face. "I get it - it's one of those 'church things', right?"
Molly squared her shoulders and looked Julie in the eye. "Could be, but then **I want things that last, don't you?"**

* * * * * * * * *

Before we write this example off as 'one of those teen-age things', let's take a closer look. Think about applying for (and keeping) a job, building relationships, and such everyday things as getting the help you need in stores, restaurants, etc..

Of course, **looking good and/or unique can get you attention,** but what about after that? It's true that other people develop first impressions based on how we look and initially behave, but what's next? Once we have attention, what do we do with it? Will it be the attention we want and/or need?

Peter is digging deeply into the bedrock of relationship with these instructions. He says, *"...let your adornment be the inner self ...."*, and, *"What matters is not your outer appearance - the styling of your hair, the jewelry you wear, the cut of your clothes - but your inner disposition."*

So sure, it's good to look nice, but what do you look like on the inside? He's warning us that **our insides will surely shine through whatever our outsides look like.** Have you ever met someone who looks really good on the outside, only to discover quickly that this is definitely not someone you want to get to know? Or perhaps you've met someone whose outer appearance almost makes you not want to meet them at all, but then you find out they're really great?

Did you know there are many people who've met "Christians" and decided they want nothing to do with any of them? It's usually not the outward appearance that turns them off, it's what shines through (or doesn't) after the first meeting. You see, **a real Christian must take the time and attention to know the real Christ at work in their real lives.** Now that's a true 'holy advantage' that outlasts and outshines any mere image the world could ever produce.

How are you feeding and growing your 'holy advantage', so that you "*...let your adornment be the inner self....*"?

In other words, do we want a worldly advantage, or a holy advantage?

Reflections

What is a "worldly advantage" like?   How about a "holy advantage"?

Have you ever met someone who looks really good on the outside, only to discover quickly that this is definitely not someone you want to get to know?

Or perhaps you've met someone whose outer appearance almost makes you not want to meet them at all, but then you find out they're really great?

Did you know there are many people who've met "Christians" and decided they want nothing to do with any of them? How has this affected your own faith life?

How are you feeding and growing your 'holy advantage', so that you "*...let your adornment be the inner self....*"?

23

Blessed Blessing

*Finally, **all of you should agree and have concern and love for each other.** You also should be kind and humble. Don't be hateful and insult people just because they are hateful and insult you. Instead, treat everyone with kindness.*

You are God's chosen ones, and he will bless you. The Scriptures say, "Do you really love life? Do you want to be happy? Then stop saying cruel things and quit telling lies. Give up your evil ways and do right, as you find and follow the road that leads to peace. The Lord watches over everyone who obeys him, and he listens to their prayers. But he opposes everyone who does evil."

Can anyone really harm you for being eager to do good deeds? Even if you have to suffer for doing good things, God will bless you. So stop being afraid about what people might do.　　　- 1 Peter 3: 8-14 (Contemporary English Version)

Summing up: Be agreeable, be sympathetic, be loving, be compassionate, be humble. That goes for all of you, no exceptions. No retaliation. No sharp-tongued sarcasm.

Instead, bless - You'll be a blessing and also get a blessing. *"Whoever wants to embrace life and see the day fill up with good, here's what you do: say nothing evil or hurtful; snub evil and cultivate good; run after peace for all you're worth. God looks on all this with approval, listening and responding well to what he's asked; but he turns his back on those who do evil things."*

If with heart and soul you're doing good, do you think you can be stopped? *Even if you suffer for it, you're still better off. Don't give the opposition a second thought.*　　　- 1 Peter 3: 8-14 (The Message Version)

* * * * * * * * * *

"Is this the Blessing House? The guy at the sandwich place told me to come here and ask you that. I know it's weird, but....." The young woman shifted her weight back and forth, left to right, right to left as she fidgeted with her long curly hair. **The big backpack seemed as if it would topple her over backwards** any time. The friendly grandmother-type lady who answered the door smiled, and the young woman looked behind herself to see who the lady was smiling at. No one there.... "Honey, welcome! It's getting a bit cold out there. Want to come in for a bit? We're all just settling in for some hot chocolate by the fireplace."

Seeing uncertainty mingled with a trace of fear in the young woman's eyes, the older woman held her hand out. "They call me Betty around here. What's your name?" More shifting, left foot to right foot, right foot to left foot. Looking Betty in the eye for the first time, she answered. "My name's Allie. Funny thing, my grandma's name was Betty...."

"How interesting. **Well, how about if we just sit here on the porch?** I'll go inside and get us some of that hot chocolate." Betty stepped back into the house, closing only the glass storm door. **Allie couldn't help herself; she stepped closer, peering in through the door. There it was** - a fireplace, complete with a roaring fire. Gathered around the fireplace she saw three, no four women, laughing and talking. Just then Betty came strolling back to the door and stepped onto the porch, two steaming mugs of chocolate in her hands.

"Isn't that backpack heavy?" Why not take it off and rest a spell? These chairs are really comfy!" Betty plopped down in one of the overstuffed porch chairs, a relaxed smile on her face. *Funny*, Allie thought, *her smile goes all the way to her eyes. I think she really means it.* So Allie dumped the backpack on the porch and let herself sink into the other porch chair. *Wow. I could stay in this chair a good long time; I could even sleep here!* It had been a long month. **Thrown out of her house, she'd been living in the park,** using the public bathroom there to wash up before school every morning.

Allie looked up at the sign by the door. Sure enough, it said 'Blessing House - Blessed to be a Blessing!'. **Betty saw her reading the sign. "Bet you're wondering what all that means, right?"** Allie nodded.

"Well, a long (but not so long) time ago, **I was somewhat like you. No place to go, thought no one cared either.** The lady that lived here, she met me in that park down the street. She took me in - hired me to stay here and clean house for her. Funny though, she only wanted it cleaned on Saturdays, and then we always cleaned together. 'Blessed to be a blessing', she used to always say, especially when I was wondering exactly what I was good for. **She taught me that everybody had a blessing, everybody mattered to God.** When I didn't believe her, that's when she told me about Jesus, about just how much God loved even me. She left this house to me - me! Only one requirement: I had to use it to be a blessing. So here we are, Allie, you and I here on this porch. Those ladies in there? Just like you, they're figuring out how God has richly blessed them. Just like you (and me), they came here thinking they weren't worth much. **So Allie, want to come in and try it out, see if the blessing fits?** No strings around here - except love maybe. How about it?"

So Allie stepped into the warm living room and into the reality of God's blessing. A year later she graduated from high school - with honors. She went to the university in town, earning a masters degree in social work, all the while living in the Blessing House. She became a part of its ministry. Allie was shocked and surprised when Betty died. Blessing House was now hers!

She had tears in her eyes as she stood to speak at Betty's funeral. Gulping back tears, she said simply this: "Blessed to be a blessing. That was Betty. That was all of us whose lives have been touched by her and Blessing House. Every time we are blessed to be a blessing, we honor her. As she always said, 'How about it?'"

* * * * * * * * *

This Scripture calls us to a difficult ministry: *"Instead, bless - You'll be a blessing and also get a blessing."* None of us is perfect, but Peter gives us goals as we grow in relationship with God through Jesus Christ, led and empowered by the Holy Spirit.

Betty and Allie were certainly not perfect people (none of us are), but they both lived with these biblical goals front-and-center in their lives.

Meditating on this Scripture can help us take stock of how we're doing with being 'blessed to be a blessing', in living in faith every day.

Let's intentionally open our eyes more fully this week to those whom God sends into our lives to share God's blessing with us!

Reflections

Go back and 'walk' through this Scripture again. What part of it catches your eye?

Pick one area you can work on this week. Pray for guidance, for God to show you how to be more of a blessing in this way. Pray for the Holy Spirit to empower you. Pray to see Christ's example of your choice every day this week. Then start each day as one who is indeed… blessed to be a blessing!

Use the space below to record your thoughts and reflections throughout this week.

24

Mud Bath!

Do not fear what they fear, and do not be intimidated, but in your hearts sanctify Christ as Lord. **Always be ready to make your defense to anyone who demands from you an accounting for the hope that is in you; yet do it with gentleness and reverence.** *Keep your conscience clear, so that, when you are maligned, those who abuse you for your good conduct in Christ may be put to shame.*

For it is better to suffer for doing good, if suffering should be God's will, than to suffer for doing evil. For Christ also suffered for sins once for all, the righteous for the unrighteous, in order to bring you to God. He was put to death in the flesh, but made alive in the spirit, in which also he went and made a proclamation to the spirits in prison, who in former times did not obey, when God waited patiently in the days of Noah, during the building of the ark, in which a few, that is, eight persons, were saved through water.

And baptism, which this prefigured, now saves you-- not as a removal of dirt from the body, but as an appeal to God for a good conscience, through the resurrection of Jesus Christ, *who has gone into heaven and is at the right hand of God, with angels, authorities, and powers made subject to him.*

- 1 Peter 3: 15-22 (New Revised Standard Version)

So don't be afraid and don't worry. Instead, you must worship Christ as Lord of your life. **And if you are asked about your Christian hope, always be ready to explain it. But you must do this in a gentle and respectful way.** *Keep your conscience clear. Then if people speak evil against you, they will be ashamed when they see what a good life you live because you belong to Christ.*

Remember, it is better to suffer for doing good, if that is what God wants, than to suffer for doing wrong! Christ also suffered when he died for our sins once for all time. He never sinned, but he died for sinners that he might bring us safely home to God. He suffered physical death, but he was raised to life in the Spirit.

So he went and preached to the spirits in prison--those who disobeyed God long ago when God waited patiently while Noah was building his boat. Only eight people were saved from drowning in that terrible flood.

And this is a picture of baptism, which now saves you by the power of Jesus Christ's resurrection. Baptism is not a removal of dirt from your body; it is an appeal to God from a clean conscience.

Now Christ has gone to heaven. He is seated in the place of honor next to God, and all the angels and authorities and powers are bowing before him.

- 1 Peter 3: 15-22 (New Living Translation)

* * * * * * * * * *

"**Daddy, why are all those people taking baths at church**....with their clothes on!?   I mean, don't they have bathtubs at their house? And they look like they're already clean!"

"Shhh!"

"But Daddy, **where's the soap?** Mommy always has a fit if I don't use soap!"

"I said SHHHH!"

"**Mommy, Mommy....why aren't they scrubbing?** You always make me scrub...everything!"

"Shhh!"

"**Mommy, did you have a church bath-tism too?**"

"Yes, honey, now SHHHH!"

"**Hey Sissy, you think they'll let me have my bath-tism at home,** in our tub? I don't wanna get all draggly-looking in front of all these people!"

Now three sets of eyes all fastened on young Bert. Not happy eyes, not at all. He got the message, but he was still confused. He looked down, thinking. His feet kicked the air as they dangled off the church pew.

Not to be deterred, as soon as worship was over (not even before the last note of the last song ended), Bert darted out of his seat, dashed down the aisle, and presented himself to the pastor at the back of the church.

"**Pastor, why did those people have their baths at church today...in front of everybody?** My mom says you should take your bath by yourself - with the door shut! And why didn't you use soap? And why didn't they scrub? And why did you call it a bath-tism? And why did they have clothes - those funny looking robe things - on?"

As Bert's questions slowed to a stop, the pastor took a deep breath to answer. By then, his mom, dad, and big sister had caught up with him. **"Sorry, Pastor," his dad began**, but Pastor Jerry interrupted him. **"No need to be sorry, Carl. Bert's got some really good questions,** and I'd like to talk to him about them. How about if we all go to the Burger Barn for lunch?"

"**Can we, dad? Can we go to the Burger Barn with Pastor Jerry?**" Excitement bubbled through Bert's young voice. Carl hesitated. "Well, Bert, we have a meeting this afternoon, and...." Pastor Jerry thought a minute. "How about this, Carl: Mary and I would love to treat Bert, and Sara here too, to a Burger Barn lunch. We can just bring them back home later. How would that be?"

So it was that Pastor Jerry, his wife Mary, Sara, and Bert had what they'd later laughingly call their **"Mud Bath Burger Barn Day"**. They all climbed into Pastor Jerry's big truck for the ride to Burger Barn.

Bert was so excited that he didn't notice the huge pothole in the parking lot - filled with mud - until he landed in it, slipped, and, well.....you can just imagine what his good Sunday clothes looked like! Sara came around the truck just in time to see Pastor Jerry pulling her little brother out of the muck and mud. She barely suppressed a giggle. What would mom say?

Well, it was a warm day, and "Mrs. Pastor" Mary didn't miss a beat. "Hey, Bert, come with me. We can fix this - at least well enough to get a burger!" With that, she reached for his hand, led him around the side of the building, turned on the hose, and hosed the mud from him. He was now dripping wet, so she took him back to the truck, opened the back, grabbed a couple of the baptismal towels, and rubbed him down.

Mary laughed, thinking of little Bert's "bath-tism" questions. **"OK, now you're a bit wet, but you sure look better than you did a few minutes ago!"** Pastor Jerry and Sara went inside to get food for all of them while Mary and Bert sat in the sunshine at one of the outdoor tables. Soon they were all happily munching on burgers and fries in the warm spring sunshine.

"Pastor Jerry? **So was that my bath-tism?** I mean, you were talking about how bath-tism washed all the dirt away, and that's about as dirty as I've ever been!"

Mary watched and waited, a twinkle in her eye. How would Jerry answer this one?

"Well Bert, what you had was a bath, well, more like a big shower with your clothes on!" They all laughed. **"But seriously Bert, what baptism does is wash dirt away from our insides."**

Now Bert was really confused. **Washing your insides? Yuk!!** I mean, he remembered when he ate some bad food...now that felt like washing his insides. Why, daddy even talked about how it 'cleaned out his insides'. No way he wanted to do that again! **"Pastor Jerry, I don't think I want my insides cleaned out - unhh unhh!"**

Mary couldn't help laughing now. "No, honey, that's not the kind of insides Pastor Jerry's talking about. I think he's talking about the kind of inside dirt like when you do something you shouldn't, and you feel all wrong inside - that kind of dirt. Is that right, Pastor Jerry?"

Jerry gave his wife an extremely thankful look. "That's exactly right, honey. But even better, it's like letting Jesus into all your messes. **Bert, when you get baptized, you say 'yes' to Jesus, and you let Him into your life so He can help you stay clean on the inside."**

Bert thought for a while. Before he could say anything though, **Sara spoke.** "You know, Pastor Jerry, I understand now. I mean, when you were talking this morning about dying to the world's dirt and rising to a new life in Christ, I almost got it. Now I get it all the way. **I need Jesus like that. Can I be baptized? I mean, is it too late?"**

Pastor Jerry had been concentrating so much on Bert that he hadn't been paying any attention to Sara. She was a very quiet, deep-thinking young lady. **"Well, Sara, do you know what it means to make Jesus the Lord of your life?"** Sara thought for a minute. "I think so. I mean, I talk to Him all the time, and I ask Him to show me the right ways to act. I ask Him for the Holy Spirit to make me strong and brave when people are doing the wrong things. **Since I'm in middle school now, I really depend on Him all the time, you know?"**

"Sounds like you're ready, Sara, and you know what?" He paused, looking her in the eye. **"It's never too late. I'll talk to your folks. Maybe we'll just have another baptism next Sunday!"**

Bert was the first one to jump out of the truck when they pulled up in their driveway. He ran over to his dad, who was pruning a bush. **"Daddy! Daddy! Guess what? Next Sunday, Sara's getting her insides cleaned out - at church!"**

＊ ＊ ＊ ＊ ＊ ＊ ＊ ＊ ＊

We all take mud baths each day - to some degree. As we live in the world, we pick up dirt and grime. In baptism, we claim Jesus the Christ as Lord of our lives. We open our hearts, minds, and lives to Him. But that's not the end. We must live in Him each day, allowing Him to, as Sara said so well, "show us the right ways and make us strong", to give us grace and courage to live through and into our identity as Christians - Christ-followers.

We all need to be able to respond , in our own way and with our own unique, God-given gifts, so that, *"... if you are asked about your Christian hope, always be ready to explain it. But you must do this in a gentle and respectful way."*

What does it mean to live life as Christ's follower, His disciple? What difference does it make in your life? How is your life blessed and strengthened by His presence in your mind, your heart, your life?

Are you letting Jesus the Christ spray the hose of grace on the mud that coats you daily in the world? I pray that you experience His grace-showers daily, and that you indeed feel cleaned - from the inside out!

Reflections

How is baptism like "getting your insides cleaned out"?

What does it mean to make Jesus the Christ "Lord of your life"?

How does our real everyday life give us "mud baths" every day?

How do we clean the grime of those "mud baths" out of our lives?

What is your response to the instruction to, *"...if you are asked about your Christian hope, always be ready to explain it. But you must do this in a gentle and respectful way."?*

25

Quick Thinking!

Christ suffered here on earth. Now you must be ready to suffer as he did, because suffering shows you have stopped sinning. It means you have turned from your own desires and want to obey God for the rest of your life. **You have already lived long enough like people who don't know God.** *You were immoral and followed your evil desires. You went around drinking and partying and carrying on. In fact, you even worshipped disgusting idols.*

Now your former friends wonder why you have stopped running around with them, *and they curse you for it. But they will have to answer to God, who judges the living and the dead. The good news has even been preached to the dead, so that after they have been judged for what they have done in this life, their spirits will live with God. Everything will soon come to an end so be serious and be sensible enough to pray.*

Most important of all, you must sincerely love each other, because love wipes away many sins. *Welcome people into your home and don't grumble about it. Each of you has been blessed with one of God's many wonderful gifts to be used in the service of others.* **So use your gift well.** *if you have the gift of speaking, preach God's message. If you have the gift of helping others, do it with the strength that God supplies.* **Everything should be done in a way that will bring honor to God because of Jesus Christ, who is glorious and powerful forever.**

- 1 Peter 4: 1-11 (Contemporary English Version)

Since Jesus went through everything you're going through and more, learn to think like him. Think of your sufferings as a weaning from that old sinful habit of always expecting to get your own way. Then you'll be able to live out your days free to pursue what God wants instead of being tyrannized by what you want. **You've already put in your time in that God-ignorant way of life,** *partying night after night, a drunken and profligate life.* **Now it's time to be done with it for good.**

Of course, your old friends don't understand why you don't join in with the old gang anymore. But you don't have to give an account to them. *They're the ones who will be called on the carpet--and before God himself. Listen to the Message. It was preached to those believers who are now dead, and yet even though they died (just as all people must), they will still get in on the life that God has given in Jesus. Everything in the world is about to be wrapped up, so take nothing for granted.* **Stay wide-awake in prayer.**

Most of all, love each other as if your life depended on it. Love makes up for practically anything. *Be quick to give a meal to the hungry, a bed to the homeless--cheerfully. Be generous with the different things God gave you, passing them around so all get in on it: if words, let it be God's words; if help, let it be God's hearty help. That way, God's bright presence will be evident in everything through Jesus, and he'll get all the credit as the One mighty in everything--encores to the end of time. Oh, yes!* -1 Peter 4: 1-11 (The Message Version)

* * * * * * * * *

The summer mission trip changed everything. How could she go back to school the same way? What would her friends say?

Shannon almost hadn't gone on that trip. Almost. But then Brad (the cutest guy in the senior class) had asked her. Shannon remembered thinking, *Wow!* **Most girls dream of a date with Brad. She'd get a whole two weeks!**

That was all before she learned who Brad really was - other than cute, that is. She hadn't even known he was religious, let alone that he belonged to a church young adult group!
So here she was - a week before the start of her senior year. **She'd just returned from the trip five days ago, and already things were different.** Not always a nice comfortable different either.

First came the call from Jennifer, one of the friends she hung out with all the time. "Hey Shannon, let's party! Toby's having a thing at his house, and it'll be a blast - kind of a senior year kick-off. Everyone'll be there, and, well, everything too, know what I mean? I know you, and I know you'll have a blast. Remember our big end of the year party last year? Well, you probably don't remember much of it anyway, but.... So, are you in?"

Well, a month ago, wild horses couldn't have kept Shannon away from that party. **But now,** well... "So Jennifer, who's coming? Do you know if Brad'll be there?"
After a second (or two) of silence, Jennifer found her voice. She chuckled, **"Shannon, he's cute, but** surely you know by now that he, well, he doesn't know how to have any real fun. Not like we do anyway, right? Know what I mean?" Getting no immediate answer, Jennifer laughed again. "Oh Shannon, you're not going out with him, are you? Seriously? Oh wow."

Shannon was stuck now. Time for some quick thinking! Would Jennifer still like her? Did it matter? (Of course it did.) Would the whole crowd want to hang out with her - or even talk to her? Would her whole senior year be ruined? This was the year she'd been planning and waiting for - forever!

"Well, Jenn, you know I just got back from that trip to Miami. **Let me get back to you;** I've got to check my work schedule, and....." She could feel Jennifer shut down, even over the phone. **"Sure Shannon, whatever.** I just hope you don't miss out, that's all." And then Jennifer just hung up! Before Shannon could even answer, Jennifer was gone.

She'd just walked into the kitchen when her phone rang. Shannon looked at the caller ID on the counter. It was Brad! Stuck between happiness (she did like him, and he was cute) and dread (would this mean the end of her old, fun life?), she let it ring a few times before answering.

"Hey Shannon, want to go out for some pizza and a movie?"

Brad came by to pick her up an hour later. **They never made it to the theater.** Instead, they spent three hours just talking at the pizza place.

As Brad drove Shannon home, they passed by Jennifer's street. "Brad, wait! Look!" Shannon pointed down Jennifer's street as they stopped at the intersection. "What are all those cops doing on....oh wow! I think they're actually at her house!" So Brad turned onto Jennifer's street and they parked a couple of houses away.

Shannon counted four police cars and two ambulances. What happened? As they got out of the car, one of the officers approached them. "You'll have to stay back," he told them, as he turned and took a step back toward the scene. Then he turned back to Brad and Shannon. "You don't live here, do you? Know any of these kids?"

Brad was quick to answer. "No, neither of us lives here, but yes, we do know someone who does. Her name is Jennifer." The policeman's face changed in an instant. Something bad had definitely happened. **"So, do either of you know how we could contact Jennifer's parents?"** Just then, Jennifer's dad drove up, stopped his car in the middle of the street, and jumped out. The officer stepped in front of him. "Sir, do you live here?" Jennifer's dad nodded, speechless. "Well, sir, I need you to come with me. Seems these kids had a party; didn't turn out too well, either. No sir, it sure didn't." The two men walked toward the house together as Brad and Shannon stood silently in the middle of the street.

"Brad, you know I could have been here. She called, and she was really ticked off when she figured out I wasn't coming. If you hadn't invited me on that trip, if you hadn't asked me out tonight, well....." Shannon turned her face from the scene at the house, tears streaming down her face. Brad turned her into his shoulder and wrapped his arms around her. **As he stood looking at Jennifer's house, he remembered the friend who'd invited him on the mission trip last year.** He remembered how he'd almost said no. He remembered his old teammate Rick, the guy he used to hang with. Rick, who'd OD'd on something at one of these 'pharm parties' last summer - Rick, who'd never see his senior year.

"Hey Shannon, let's go, OK? We can stop by in a couple of days, see if we can help her folks. Remember what that street kid said in Miami? I think this is it: **'Jesus gives you a new life. Think quick and grab it,** then live it for Him, even if your old life doesn't get it - <u>especially</u> if your old life doesn't get it.'" Shannon stepped back to look at him. "You know Brad, I invited Jenn to come too, but she said no. I wish she'd said yes."

✳ ✳ ✳ ✳ ✳ ✳ ✳ ✳ ✳

Christ invites us to a new life each and every day. He invites us to set aside some part of our 'old' lives and replace it with His newness. The trouble is, the more we say 'no' to Him, the less we even notice His invitations. On the other hand though, the more we invite Christ into our 'old' lives, the newer and stronger our lives grow and the more living with Him becomes as natural as breathing! Our 'old' lives look more and more foreign to us - as our relationship with God more and more defines who we are.

Life can be newer, stronger, and more joyful each day. Yes, sometimes we will fail, but we must begin again each day. God will never abandon us! We can choose to take small steps each day to allow Christ more fully into our lives. What will that step be today? Will we, like Brad and his friend, invite someone else to join us on the journey?

Reflections

What came to mind as you read, "Christ invites us to a new life each and every day." And "Life can be newer, stronger, and more joyful each day."?

Reflections (continued)

What small steps can you make to allow Christ more fully into your life today? Tomorrow?

26

A Refinery...Here?

Beloved, do not be surprised at the fiery ordeal that is taking place among you to test you, as though something strange were happening to you. But rejoice insofar as you are sharing Christ's sufferings, so that you may also be glad and shout for joy when his glory is revealed.

If you are reviled for the name of Christ, you are blessed, because the spirit of glory, which is the Spirit of God, is resting on you. But let none of you suffer as a murderer, a thief, a criminal, or even as a mischief maker.

Yet if any of you suffers as a Christian, do not consider it a disgrace, but glorify God because you bear this name. For the time has come for judgment to begin with the household of God; if it begins with us, what will be the end for those who do not obey the gospel of God? And "If it is hard for the righteous to be saved, what will become of the ungodly and the sinners?"

Therefore, let those suffering in accordance with God's will entrust themselves to a faithful Creator, while continuing to do good.
                                                    - 1 Peter 4: 12-19 (New Revised Standard Version)

Dear friends, don't be surprised at the fiery trials you are going through, as if something strange were happening to you. Instead, be very glad-- because these trials will make you partners with Christ in his suffering, and afterward you will have the wonderful joy of sharing his glory when it is displayed to all the world.

Be happy if you are insulted for being a Christian, for then the glorious Spirit of God will come upon you. If you suffer, however, it must not be for murder, stealing, making trouble, or prying into other people's affairs.

But it is no shame to suffer for being a Christian. Praise God for the privilege of being called by his wonderful name! For the time has come for judgment, and it must begin first among God's own children. And if even we Christians must be judged, what terrible fate awaits those who have never believed God's Good News? And "If the righteous are barely saved, what chance will the godless and sinners have?"

So if you are suffering according to God's will, keep on doing what is right, and trust yourself to the God who made you, for he will never fail you.
                                                    - 1 Peter 4: 12-19 (New Living Translation)

* * * * * * * * *

"So tell me again, why is this house so much less than the one on the next street? I mean, it's got more square footage, it's cleaner, and the yard, well, it's fantastic!" Aaron still couldn't believe it - this house was **a full $8000 less expensive** than the other one! His wife looked again at the real estate listing. They both turned to the real estate agent. "Well....," he began, **"It is right next door to the church, and, well, it's not just any church.** They're always doing things there - lots of comings and goings, that sort of thing."

Lila finally spoke up. **"Aren't there supposed to be things going on at churches?** I mean, classes, worship, meetings, things like that? What could be so bad about that?" They looked at the realtor again. Aaron could tell there was more to this 'next door to the church' thing than they were thinking. Neither of them had been to church since they were kids, but how different could this church be? "It looks like a nice little church," Lila began. As they stood on the home's front porch, she looked at the church. "And it's kept up really well. They've got trimmed bushes, nice flower gardens, and a good parking lot. What goes on there that you think we should be concerned about?"

The realtor took a deep breath. **"Well, see the church sign? It says 'Neighborhood Spirit-Refinery'. I guess that pretty much says it.** Puzzled looks from both Aaron and Lila let him know he'd have to say more. "OK, here's the thing. That church, **it's always doing something.** Parking lot concerts, neighborhood cleanups, community gardening, seminars on just about everything - kids, parenting, senior issues, caregivers, - oh, and health fairs too. I shouldn't forget they shelter the homeless every weekend either. Yep, Friday and Saturday nights about thirty homeless folks stay there. They do big 'Prayer Walk' events too."

Lila thought she was getting it. **"So they go around knocking on doors asking people if they're saved and stuff?"** The realtor laughed. "Nope, they just walk through different neighborhoods praying quietly for people, that's all. I suppose if someone asked them about it, they'd talk, but no, they're not the 'if you died today, where would you go' kind, no. Oh, and I almost forgot. They have kids' camp all summer, and a Bible study group that meets all year. In warm weather they meet in that picnic area over there." He pointed to the tables on the side of the church. **"See those barbeque pits?** They're smokin' just about every Saturday, and guess what? They just give the food away! Anybody can come, eat, and just hang out. Can you imagine what that nice peaceful parking lot looks like then?"

A big grin blossomed on Aaron's face. **"Free barbeque every Saturday? Wow!"** He could just taste it now. Lila was getting excited too. Summer camp - right next door? And parenting classes? Hey, I like this house more and more!"

The realtor gave them that 'you don't get it' look. "Aaron, Lila, but see, the parking lot's always full, and they'll park in front of your place too. That was a big deal to the Ramirez's. Why they even went to City Hall about it - a few times - and they called the police all the time too. They made it real hard for the church to go on doing all that stuff....why, **I heard they were even talking about having to move the church!"**

"What for? I mean, nothing you've mentioned sounds that dangerous or loud, or...." **Just then a couple walked across the church parking lot toward them.** The woman approached them and held out her hand. "Hi, I'm Melinda. We go to the church next door. You thinking of buying the house? I mean, we don't want to interrupt or anything..."

Lila reached out and shook the woman's hand. "I'm Lila, and this is my husband Aaron. **Can you tell me about your church sign? I mean, it IS a bit unusual - "Neighborhood Spirit-Refinery", right?"**

Melinda smiled. "This is my friend Jacob. **I guess you could say we grow spirits at our church.** We just help each other grow closer to God and live more like Jesus said He wants us to. So we try to let Him out as much as we can." Jacob added, **"The 'refining' part just means we try to help each other get the junk out of our lives so there's more room for God.** Oh, and it's not some kind of secret club either. We go all out to be sure that anyone who's human and not perfect - like us - knows they can come just as they are. Now Jesus might not leave them that way, but...." He laughed. "Anyway, that's the exciting part. Can we answer any other questions?"

Aaron looked at Lila. Lila looked at Aaron. They turned as one to the realtor. Aaron spoke first. "I think this house is perfect. **We'd love living next to a refinery, right honey?"** Lila smiled at their new friends Jacob and Melinda. "Oh yeah, and our kids are going to love this! Is there a barbeque this Saturday? We love to barbeque. **Can we help?"**

* * * * * * * * *

Listen to another voice from Scripture:
"For he will be like a blazing fire that refines metal or like a strong soap that whitens clothes. He will sit and *judge like a refiner of silver,* **watching closely as the dross is burned away.** *He will purify the Levites, refining them like gold or silver, so that they may once again offer acceptable sacrifices to the LORD."* - Malachi 3:2b-3 (New Living Translation)

We don't always like the thought of being 'refined', especially when it involves imagery of a 'blazing fire'! But sometimes there are parts of our lives that need to be changed, things we need to eliminate in order for God to enter our lives and more completely work in and through us. We need to be refined.

Our churches should all be places such as the one in this story. Could your church (or one you know of) be called a "Spirit-Refinery"? Are you willing to allow God to get to work "refining" you? Think about it. What would your life be like if you were truly close to God - if you could experience the Holy Spirit moving in your life every day? What if you truly felt Jesus guiding you, as close to you as your next breath?

How would it be to feel like "pure gold or silver" in God's eyes?

Can you say 'yes' to God's request to put a "Spirit-Refinery" in your neighborhood? In your heart?

Reflections

How would you feel about living next door to the church in this story?

If you are involved in a church, how does it compare to the "Neighborhood Spirit-Refinery" church?

If you participate in a church community, how are you a part of increasing its vitality and connection with people?

27

Real Jesus - Real Church

I have a special concern for you church leaders. I know what it's like to be a leader, in on Christ's sufferings as well as the coming glory. Here's my concern: that you care for God's flock with all the diligence of a shepherd. Not because you have to, but because you want to please God. Not calculating what you can get out of it, but acting spontaneously.[Not bossily telling others what to do, but tenderly showing them the way.

When God, who is the best shepherd of all, comes out in the open with his rule, he'll see that you've done it right and commend you lavishly. And you who are younger must follow your leaders. **But all of you, leaders and followers alike, are to be down to earth with each other,** *for God has had it with the proud, but* **takes delight in just plain people.** *So be content with who you are, and don't put on airs.*

God's strong hand is on you; he'll promote you at the right time. Live carefree before God; he is most careful with you. Keep a cool head. Stay alert. The Devil is poised to pounce, and would like nothing better than to catch you napping. Keep your guard up.

You're not the only ones plunged into these hard times. It's the same with Christians all over the world. So keep a firm grip on the faith. *The suffering won't last forever. It won't be long before this generous God who has great plans for us in Christ--eternal and glorious plans they are! -* **will have you put together and on your feet for good. He gets the last word; yes, he does.**

I'm sending this brief letter to you by Silas, a most dependable brother. I have the highest regard for him. I've written as urgently and accurately as I know how. **This is God's generous truth; embrace it with both arms!** *The church in exile here with me--but not for a moment forgotten by God--wants to be remembered to you. Mark, who is like a son to me, says hello. Give holy embraces all around! Peace to you--to all who walk in Christ's ways.*

- 1 Peter 5: 1-14 (The Message Version)

* * * * * * * * *

"A leader? Me? No way!" This was the young man's response to the debate seminar presenter's statement that everyone is a leader in some way every day. Her eyebrows went up as she heard his response. **"Toby, what makes you think no one follows you?"**

"Well, Ms.," he glanced at her nametag. "Ms. Mortons, at work I serve restaurant customers. At home I try to do what my folks tell me. At school, well, at school the teachers and principals and **all of them are in charge. They're the leaders, not me. And you know, I kind of like it that way a lot of the time."**

Ms. Mortons smiled. **"Well, let's all look at Toby's situation.** That OK, Toby?" He nodded, leaning forward. She glanced around the room. All twenty pair of eyes were now paying full attention. After all, this was their world she was talking about, and they knew Toby. Most of them had been in speech and debate classes together all through their high school years. As seniors in this advanced placement debate course, leadership was a hot topic of conversation.

"We'll start by looking at each of the places he mentioned. First, Toby, you said that 'At work, I serve restaurant customers.' Is that right?" He nodded. "Do they ever ask you questions about the menu - you know, what's good that day, or how much food is in a dish, or....I could go on, right?" Several heads nodded. She looked around the room. "So let's ask ourselves this: why would they ask Toby? I mean, are they looking for guidance to make good choices?"

Belinda, sitting in the front row, raised her hand. **"I think I get it! Whenever he guides a customer to make choices, he's leading them...?"** Ms. Mortons nodded. "That's right. By the way, how long have you worked at the diner, Toby?" Still looking a bit unsure, he answered, "Three years. I'll be quitting next month to go to K State."

"I see. Any new servers at the diner say, in the last year?" He nodded yes. "Well, you ever help them out, I mean answer their questions, show them how to do anything, things like that?"
Toby smiled. "OK, I get it. You mean that each time I help someone make a decision or help train a new server I'm acting like a leader. Is that it?" Belinda spoke up again, this time so excited she forgot to raise her hand. **"No Toby, not *acting like* a leader. You *are* a leader."**

"So let's look at Toby's next , we'll call them his 'theaters of influence'. **He told us, 'At home, I try to do what my folks tell me.' That about right?"** He nodded again, *very* interested in what she'd do with *this* one. "You're going to K State, right?" Toby nodded, really confused. *What could that have to do with anything?*

"How did you come to that decision? I mean did your folks do all the research, go visit campuses, and then tell you where you were going? I suppose that could happen, but...." Laughter bubbled through the group. Brent, a tall young man in the back, spoke up. "This group is pretty, well, self-directed I'd call it. Yeah, right, I can just see that scenario....not!"

Ms. Mortons smiled broadly. This was a great group of young people! **"So how did that work for all of you?"** They talked for quite a while about all the research these seniors had done, how they'd worked out final choices, and how the final college choices had been made. "So what I hear you saying is that in many ways you had a lot to teach your parents about these colleges and the overall process of choosing, right?"

Toby raised his hand. "OK, you've got me again. So what you're saying is that in lots of ways I led my folks in learning about colleges and the whole rat race of picking one. It'll sure be a lot easier for my little sister in a couple of years..." He chuckled. **"You don't even have to say it. I'm leading my little sister too, right? Even though she's a real pain sometimes."**

Brent spoke up again. **"Ms. Mortons, I *really* want to hear about this school thing.** I mean, you truly think we're leaders around here?" Tisha, silent until now, spoke up before Ms. Mortons had a chance. "Well, yeah! Duh, remember when they wanted to rip out all the trees and stuff to put in more parking lots or something? We made all those phone calls, we went to the city council, we got the newspaper and the TV stations out here - remember that? I don't see any parking lot out there now, do you? That's leadership. Right Ms. Mortons?"

"Wow, just wow." Toby shook his head. "This class is so cool. **I never, ever thought we were leaders, you know, real leaders.** Adults like to say things like 'You're the leaders of the future!', stuff like that. Makes you think you're nothing right now, but that's not right. **We're all leaders sometime, someplace, a lot more than we think.**"

✳ ✳ ✳ ✳ ✳ ✳ ✳ ✳ ✳

"We're all sheep from the front and shepherds from the back." Mike Breen, pastor and author of <u>LifeShapes</u> (a Bible and discipleship study), said. He's right. **Real followers of Jesus live and follow Him in the midst of a very real world. Real Jesus; real church.**

Listen again:
"But all of you, leaders and followers alike, are to be down to earth with each other, for--God has had it with the proud, But takes delight in just plain people...You're not the only ones plunged into these hard times. It's the same with Christians all over the world."

How is Jesus real to you? Is He a 'just on Sundays (or just at Easter and Christmas)' leader for you? Do you allow Him into your real, everyday life?

One of the things that helps us keep and grow the presence of Jesus the Christ in our real, daily lives is studying Scripture and being with other Christ-followers. They keep us real. In those times when we're not sure just how to be 'real', these companions on the journey will help us, support us, and yes, value our help and support too! We truly are "sheep from the front and shepherds from the back"!

Real Jesus. Real church. Real followers (that's us).

And oh yes, always remember: *"...keep a firm grip on the faith...He gets the last word; yes, he does... Peace to you--to all who walk in Christ's ways."*

Reflections

How are we all "sheep from the front and shepherds from the back"?

Name the places in your life where you're a leader.

Reflections (continued)

Where are you a follower?

How is Jesus real to you?

What would you say to someone who only attends church on special days such as Easter and Christmas?

Second Peter

28

Grace Leak!

Simeon Peter, a servant and apostle of Jesus Christ, To those who have received a faith as precious as ours through the righteousness of our God and Savior Jesus Christ: **May grace and peace be yours in abundance in the knowledge of God and of Jesus our Lord.**

His divine power has given us everything needed for life and godliness, through the knowledge of him who called us by his own glory and goodness. *Thus he has given us, through these things, his precious and very great promises, so that through them you may escape from the corruption that is in the world because of lust, and may become participants of the divine nature.*

For this very reason, you must make every effort to support your faith *with goodness, and goodness with knowledge, and knowledge with self-control, and self-control with endurance, and endurance with godliness, and godliness with mutual affection, and mutual affection with love.*

For if these things are yours and are increasing among you, they keep you from being ineffective and unfruitful in the knowledge of our Lord Jesus Christ. *For anyone who lacks these things is short-sighted and blind, and is forgetful of the cleansing of past sins.*

- 2 Peter 1: 1-9 (New Revised Standard Version)

From Simon Peter, a servant and an apostle of Jesus Christ. To everyone who shares with us in the privilege of believing that our God and Savior Jesus Christ will do what is just and fair. **I pray that God will be kind to you and will let you live in perfect peace! May you keep learning more and more about God and our Lord Jesus.**

We have everything we need to live a life that pleases God. It was all given to us by God's own power, *when we learned that he had invited us to share in his wonderful goodness. God made great and marvelous promises, so that his nature would become part of us. Then we would escape our evil desires and the corrupt influences of this world.*

Do your best to improve your faith. *You can do this by adding goodness, understanding, self-control, patience, devotion to God, concern for others, and love.*

If you keep growing in this way, it will show that what you know about our Lord Jesus Christ has made your lives useful and meaningful. *But if you don't grow, you are like someone who is nearsighted or blind, and you have forgotten that your past sins are forgiven.*

- 2 Peter 1: 1-9 (Contemporary English Version)

* * * * * * * * * *

Picture a third grade classroom in a local public school. The science lesson for today was about volume. The teacher had water, a pitcher, and a balloon. **Students gathered around the science table,** excited to see what would happen next (third graders tend to love messy experiments).

The teacher poured water into the pitcher slowly. **"How much water do you think this pitcher will hold?",** he asked. "A bunch - it's big!", came the first response. A small boy's freckled face wrinkled up in concentration, "Well, it says........eight cups. Wow, that IS a lot!" They all watched as, sure enough, the teacher filled the pitcher up to the top mark - eight cups.

All eyes turned to the balloon lying on the science table. It didn't look that big.... "So kids, how much water do you think <u>this</u> can hold?" He held up the balloon. The same eager 'first responder' spoke right up. "Just a teensy bit - it's small!" Then came a whole discussion about filling (and throwing) water balloons. After all, it was late spring. With school scheduled to be out in just a few weeks, thoughts had already turned to summer fun.

The teacher pulled a special "balloon filler" syringe out of the drawer and loaded it with water from the pitcher. "Who thinks all this water - eight cups, was it? **Who thinks all of it will fit in this small balloon?"** Silence descended on the group as they though and figured, figured and thought. Eyes darted back and forth between the balloon and the pitcher. Finally, three hands went up.

"OK, so who thinks.....half of the water will fit? Let's see, half of eight is.....?" "FOUR!" came the chorus of young voices. This time hands went up faster - five of them. The teacher laughed.

"All right then. Who thinks this will just be a big mess, and not much water at all will get into this balloon?" Most of the rest of the class raised their hands.

The stage was now set for the finale. **The teacher fitted the balloon over the end of the big lab syringe. He held them together and....pushed the plunger.** In went the water! Not a leak in sight! "Whew! Well kids, that's half a cup." He refilled the syringe, fitted it to the balloon again, and pushe. "Let's see, half a cup and half a cup equals......?" "A whole cup!" came the excited response. **Now every student wanted a front row view.** Kids in the back row climbed on chairs to see what would happen next.

Four more times Mr. Stevens filled the syringe, fitted it to the balloon, and pushed. The students held their breath, eyes getting bigger as the water expanded the balloon more and more. Would it pop? Would the balloon pop off the syringe and send water squirting all over the place? Resting the balloon on the science table as he pushed the last of the water in, the teacher looked up (while holding that balloon tightly!).

"So is that all? Let's see....we've got two half-cups - that's one cup. Then we put four more half-cups in here. Four halves are the same as...." One lone voice spoke up. "Two cups, and with that other cup, that's three cups in there!" "That's right," the teacher answered, looking at the pitcher, **"but we've still got more water - five cups to get in here. Think it'll fit?"**

"Who thinks it's going to explode?" Almost all the hands quickly went up. "OK then, let's do it!" As he filled up the syringe again and fitted the balloon around it, a new voice cut into the silent anticipation. "I didn't raise MY hand, Mr. Stevens. Know why? 'Cause **I think it'll fit, that's why. Bet you can't guess how I know, can you?"** Expecting a science whiz kind of answer (this kid loved science), the teacher nodded. "Sure, Todd, why do you think it'll all fit?"

Todd motioned Mr. Stevens down closer and whispered, **"Well, if you gotta know, it's like Jesus. He's real big, but once He's in your heart and you keep listening to Him, He just sort of makes your heart real big, and sometimes you're so happy you think you'll just explode!** I know I'm not supposed to talk about that in school, but you asked!" Todd's eyes twinkled as he laughed. "And you know what else? Jesus is supposed to leak - He's supposed to leak out all over everybody! Now how cool is that?" With that, Mr. Stevens almost forgot he was holding onto that balloon - almost.

Then he went back to filling the balloon. And guess what? All the water fit!

* * * * * * * * *

"...you must make every effort to support your faith with goodness, and goodness with knowledge, and knowledge with self-control, and self-control with endurance, and endurance with godliness, and godliness with mutual affection, and mutual affection with love.

For if these things are yours and are increasing among you, they keep you from being ineffective and unfruitful in the knowledge of our Lord Jesus Christ."

If we are to be truly a people who have *"...grace and peace be yours in abundance in the knowledge of God and of Jesus our Lord. "*, we must fill our hearts just like young Todd explained to his teacher that day in science class. We must continually draw the eight things this Scripture lists into our hearts:
- faith
- goodness
- knowledge
- self-control
- endurance
- godliness
- mutual affection
- love

As our hearts expand with these, we will experience so much grace and peace that we'll spring 'grace leaks' everywhere we go and in every company we keep!

We'll experience such an abundant spiritual life that we'll bear amazing fruit as we serve Christ as His effective witnesses. So fill your heart up - and may grace leak out of you....everywhere!!

Reflections

Think about the eight things listed above. How are they connected? How are they reflected in your life? In the life of your family? Your church?

- faith

Reflections (continued)

- goodness

- knowledge

- self-control

- endurance

- godliness

- mutual affection

- love

Reflections (continued)

How does God's grace "leak" out of others into your life?

How do you think grace "leaks" out of you to others?

29

Key Witness

*Therefore, brothers and sisters, **be all the more eager to confirm your call and election,** for if you do this, you will never stumble. For in this way, entry into the eternal kingdom of our Lord and Savior Jesus Christ will be richly provided for you.*

***Therefore I intend to keep on reminding you of these things,** though you know them already and are established in the truth that has come to you. **I think it right, as long as I am in this body, to refresh your memory,** since I know that my death will come soon, as indeed our Lord Jesus Christ has made clear to me.*

And I will make every effort so that after my departure you may be able at any time to recall these things. *- 2 Peter 1: 10-15 (New Revised Standard Version)*

*So, friends, **confirm God's invitation to you, his choice of you. Don't put it off; do it now. Do this, and you'll have your life on a firm footing,** the streets paved and the way wide open into the eternal kingdom of our Master and Savior, Jesus Christ.*

*Because the stakes are so high, even though you're up-to-date on all this truth and practice it inside and out, **I'm not going to let up for a minute in calling you to attention before it.** This is the post to which I've been assigned-- **keeping you alert with frequent reminders**--and I'm sticking to it as long as I live. I know that I'm to die soon; the Master has made that quite clear to me.*

And so I am especially eager that you have all this down in black and white so that after I die, you'll have it for ready reference. *- 2 Peter 1: 10-15 (The Message Version)*

* * * * * * * * * *

It had started simply enough. Out for his usual evening walking the dog, Kent looked down the alley (like usual) and witnessed a murder. Frozen in place (surely those weren't really guns - in his neighborhood) the sound of the shots left no doubt and started him running back to his apartment faster than he ever thought he could move.

He automatically dialed 9-1-1. No, he told the emergency operator, no he didn't want to give his name. No, he didn't want to give his address. Were they crazy? These people had guns! Before long his doorbell rang though. He looked through the viewhole in the front door to see a police officer. Great. Just great. How did they find him? Oh yeah, he forgot to block his number when he called. Terrific (not). Soon the guys with guns would be looking for him!

That was how it all began. As it turned out, Kent had witnessed a "drug and gang related shooting", as they put it. Drugs and gangs - in his neighborhood? "Don't you want to help?", they'd asked him. Kent remembered telling them surely there was someone else, surely....but no, apparently not. The police had been trying to catch these guys for a long time. Now the police and district attorney saw him as the perfect tool to put them away. **Two of the men had been arrested. Would Kent come down and see if he could identify them?**

Assured that he couldn't be seen, Kent had agreed. He was unprepared for the fear he felt as he looked through the one-way glass and saw them. "Yes, that's two of them," he said as memories of that day in the alley flooded his mind, "Can I go now?" That was when they'd told him. He wasn't safe. There had been another witness. Had been. Great; just great. The other witness was now in the city morgue. Before he knew it, the assistant district attorney and more detectives came in.

"You're not safe," they told him. *Well, duh!* **"You're our only key witness now.** We need you to testify against these two, and maybe you can help us identify the other guy who was with them in the alley. We think he's the boss, one of the gang leaders. You see, it's a turf war between rival drug gangs." *Was this a bad dream? Maybe if I just blink a few times, I'll be back in my apartment....but no.*

"We can protect you. We'll relocate you, change your name." They sounded so sure. But Kent was a teacher. How hidden was that? "So while you're hiding me, how am I supposed to keep my job. I'm a teacher, you know - going on eighteen years now. What about that?" Silence. Guess they hadn't figured that into their big plans.

So here he was. The school district had been very understanding, eager even, for "one of their own", as the superintendent had put it, to play such a big part in getting drug-dealing gang members off the neighborhood streets. They'd moved him to a 'safe house', as they called it. Kent's dog Minnie didn't think it was so safe. He knew she could tell Kent was afraid - always afraid. Working from his new 'home', he tracked chat room interactions looking for online predators. The only good thing about it was he actually made more money now than he did teaching, but he really missed the classroom.

The district attorney's voice snapped his attention back to the present. Hard to believe that an entire year had passed since that fateful dog-walking evening. "What did you say? I'm sorry, Mr. Yin. This is really hard for me. Will I ever have a life again - a real life?" Kent didn't see himself as a whiner, but lately.....

"Mr. Newley, you're our key witness. We just need to go over what you saw one more time, OK?" *One more time? Try about the zillionth time. Will this ever end?* "OK. Whatever you say." "Well, sir, we need your testimony to be so automatic that you are absolutely consistent, even when the other lawyer questions you. This is for you, to help you. OK?" *OK already. If I hear 'OK?' one more time, I think I'll....oh never mind.*

* * * * * * * * *

*"So, friends, **confirm God's invitation to you, his choice of you. Don't put it off; do it now. Do this, and you'll have your life on a firm footing,** ....   Because the stakes are so high, even though you're up-to-date on all this truth and practice it inside and out, **I'm not going to let up for a minute in calling you to attention before it.** .....--keeping you alert with frequent reminders--"*

As "key witnesses" to the Good News of Christ, we are called to prepare and stay connected to the reality of the Holy Spirit's work through, in, and around us. We are to keep ourselves on a "firm footing" as the Scripture says, ever alert to the forces at work in the world which seek to undermine the reality of Christ. There are spiritual drug-dealing gangs at work all around us, dealing the 'drugs' of false idols and all things against Him! **The stakes are so high that we can't even fully comprehend them.** Peter calls us to keep our relationship with God in Christ alive, vibrant, and up-to-date, practicing the Truth, the Way, and the Life each day, "inside and out".

Maintaining a strong prayer life, relationships with other Christians, and spending time and attention in Scripture all keep us alert with nourishment in this eternal spiritual battle, reminding us of who and Whose we are.

We are Christ-followers. We are disciples of Christ. We are....key witnesses!

Have you thought about the difference Christ makes in your life? Can you tell your story? How would you serve as one of His key witnesses, to both the forces of evil at work around you and the Power of the Holy Spirit working through you?

God created us each to uniquely serve the Kingdom as witnesses.
How's your key witness preparation coming?

Pray.
Be in community with other disciples of Christ, worshipping and learning.
Spend time in Scripture - and time sharing your experiences with others.
May God richly bless and enrich your spirit as His key witness!

Reflections

Have you thought about the difference Christ makes in your life? What's the story of the difference Christ has made and continues to make in your life?

How would you serve as one of His key witnesses, to both the forces of evil at work around you and the Power of the Holy Spirit working through you? How are you doing with this?

30

Light-Weight

*For we did not follow cleverly devised myths when we made known to you the power and coming of our Lord Jesus Christ, but **we had been eyewitnesses of his majesty**. For he received honor and glory from God the Father when that voice was conveyed to him by the Majestic Glory, saying, "This is my Son, my Beloved, with whom I am well pleased."*

***We ourselves heard this voice come from heaven, while we were with him on the holy mountain.** So we have the prophetic message more fully confirmed.*

*You will do well to **be attentive to this as to a lamp shining in a dark place,** until the day dawns and the morning star rises in your hearts. First of all you must understand this, that no prophecy of scripture is a matter of one's own interpretation, because **no prophecy ever came by human will, but men and women moved by the Holy Spirit spoke from God.**   - 2 Peter 1: 16-21 (New Revised Standard Version)*

*For we were not making up clever stories when we told you about the powerful coming of our Lord Jesus Christ. **We saw his majestic splendor with our own eyes** when he received honor and glory from God the Father. The voice from the majestic glory of God said to him, "This is my dearly loved Son, who brings me great joy."*

***We ourselves heard that voice from heaven when we were with him on the holy mountain.** Because of that experience, we have even greater confidence in the message proclaimed by the prophets.*

*You must pay close attention to what they wrote, for **their words are like a lamp shining in a dark place**-until the Day dawns, and Christ the Morning Star shines in your hearts. Above all, you must realize that **no prophecy in Scripture ever came from the prophet's own understanding, or from human initiative. No, those prophets were moved by the Holy Spirit, and they spoke from God.**   - 2 Peter 1: 16-21 (New Living Translation)*

* * * * * * * * * *

"Yahhhh! My eyes!" That was the universal response as we emerged from a dim candlelight prayer service into the brightness of the church lobby. Squeezing her eyes shut, our Kenyan guest exclaimed, "That light, it is....heavy!" Seeing our confusion, she laughed. "Have I chosen the wrong word? **What I think is that this world-light is so heavy, and the Holy Spirit light in the worship-room was so....so light!** You understand?"

Kiki's host 'sister' nodded. "How cool is that? I get it. **I never thought of it that way before, Kiki, but what you said, it just makes me want to go back in there and get some more of that Light-weight!"**

Kiki's face got really serious. **"My brother, he's on a mission to Congo. He could use some of this 'Light-weight', like you call it.** Brenda, can we go back in the church where the Light is and pray for him?" So we went back into the sanctuary to pray. One of the ministers came and prayed for Kiki's brother with us. Amazingly, the word must have spread, because soon more people came in to join us. We spent another hour lifting Kiki's brother Bano in prayer, as well as all those he was in ministry with in Congo. What a powerful time that was!

Several days later at a youth gathering, we began with a time of prayer for one another. Kiki spoke first. "You will not believe this, but I got an email message from my brother. At the very time we were called to prayer for him, he was in danger. Know what he told me? He said, 'Sister, I felt the words 'Light-weight' sounding in my sprit. What is that, sister?' So I wrote back and told him of our prayer meeting. He is safe for now, and thanks us for our Light-weight prayers for him."

Kiki only stayed with us for a month, but God's ministry through her was amazing. "Light-weight" soon became a common term among the youth. After one of the youth leaders spoke in worship, many others in the congregation began sharing the Light-weight (or the lack of it) in their own lives. Soon we were celebrating the presence of Light-weight in the midst of challenging times as we lifted prayers in worship together. What awesome power that Light-weight brought into our midst!

* * * * * * * * *

*"You will do well to **be attentive to this as to a lamp shining in a dark place,** until the day dawns and the morning star rises in your hearts."*

How attentive are we to the Holy Spirit shining holy light into our dark places? As a friend once said so well, "You can't eat the food until you know it's there." First we have to see the 'Light-weight' God is constantly offering us. Then we need to accept it and take it in. As we take it in, we will truly experience the gift and strength of God's 'Light-weight' in our lives!

Take some time today to lift up your worries, fears, and all those 'dark places' to God. Ask God to show you the 'Light-weight' trying to break into those places. Then take time each day to invite more and more 'Light-weight' into your everyday life!

Reflections

Think of a dark time in your life. How did 'Light-weight' shine on you during that time?

Why is it difficult for us to even see God's 'Light-weight' sometimes?

31

Downhill Slide

But there were also false prophets in Israel, just as there will be false teachers among you. *They will cleverly teach destructive heresies and* **even deny the Master who bought them.** *In this way, they will bring sudden destruction on themselves. Many will follow their evil teaching and shameful immorality.* **And because of these teachers, the way of truth will be slandered. In their greed they will make up clever lies to get hold of your money.** *But God condemned them long ago, and their destruction will not be delayed. For God did not spare even the angels who sinned. He threw them into hell, in gloomy pits of darkness, where they are being held until the day of judgment. And God did not spare the ancient world-except for Noah and the seven others in his family. Noah warned the world of God's righteous judgment. So God protected Noah when he destroyed the world of ungodly people with a vast flood. Later, God condemned the cities of Sodom and Gomorrah and turned them into heaps of ashes. He made them an example of what will happen to ungodly people.*

But God also rescued Lot out of Sodom because he was a righteous man who was sick of the shameful immorality of the wicked people around him. Yes, Lot was a righteous man who was tormented in his soul by the wickedness he saw and heard day after day.

So you see, **the Lord knows how to rescue godly people from their trials,** *even while keeping the wicked under punishment until the day of final judgment.*
- 2 Peter 2: 1-9 (New Living Translation)

But there were also lying prophets among the people then, just as there will be lying religious teachers among you. They'll smuggle in destructive divisions, pitting you against each other--biting the hand of the One who gave them a chance to have their lives back!

They've put themselves on a **fast downhill slide to destruction,** *but not before they recruit a crowd of mixed-up followers who can't tell right from wrong. They give the way of truth a bad name. They're only out for themselves. They'll say anything, anything, that sounds good to exploit you. They won't, of course, get by with it. They'll come to a bad end, for God has never just stood by and let that kind of thing go on. God didn't let the rebel angels off the hook, but jailed them in hell till Judgment Day. Neither did he let the ancient ungodly world off. He wiped it out with a flood, rescuing only eight people--Noah, the sole voice of righteousness, was one of them. God decreed destruction for the cities of Sodom and Gomorrah. A mound of ashes was all that was left--grim warning to anyone bent on an ungodly life.*

But that good man Lot, driven nearly out of his mind by the sexual filth and perversity, was rescued. Surrounded by moral rot day after day after day, that righteous man was in constant torment.

So **God knows how to rescue the godly from evil trials.** *And he knows how to hold the feet of the wicked to the fire until Judgment Day.*
- 2 Peter 2: 1-9 (The Message Version)

* * * * * * * * *

First it was the new carpet. The church had received a large sum of money to 'redo' the sanctuary and landscaping. Should the carpet be green? blue? earth tones? **That's where the trouble began.** Each carpet color seemed to have a fan club.

Then came the seating selection dilemma. What style? What color? Should the chairs be soft? firm? Should they hook together? Oh yes, and....what color? You guessed it - each had its own fan club.

Not to be outdone in divisiveness, the church grounds team tried to decide what kind of bushes should replace the (really awful looking) evergreen "sticker-things", as the preschoolers called them. Should they be more evergreens, or maybe some evergreen and some deciduous? Should they be short, tall, medium, or a combination? Flowering? Oh, did I mention that each choice had its own fan club?

The talk started out civil enough, but then....well then came some interesting campaign strategies. One man claimed that the carpet should be the closest to the "streets of gold" spoken of in Revelation 22! That would be, of course the gold/earth tone carpet.

That started a trend. Soon the proponent of the chairs that hook together referred to 1 Corinthians 12. She said that if the Body of Christ was one, the chairs should all be able to join together!

Not to be outdone, the chair of the grounds team cited the death and resurrection of Christ as his foundation for choosing flowering deciduous bushes! (They lose their leaves - 'dying' - each winter and bloom and leaf out 'resurrection' each spring.)

Soon no one could agree on anything. Comments such as these could often be overheard:
"I'm finding a church where people can agree."
"This place is crazy!"
"Where's God in this, anyway?"
"Who cares whether the chairs hook together or not?"

The pastor left. The administrative assistant left. Worship attendance dropped, and dropped.....

"But there were also lying prophets among the people then, just as there will be lying religious teachers among you. ***They'll smuggle in destructive divisions, pitting you against each other--****biting the hand of the One who gave them a chance to have their lives back!*
They've put themselves on a ***fast downhill slide to destruction,*** *but not before they recruit a crowd of mixed-up followers who can't tell right from wrong."*

* * * * * * * * *

"Lower your monthly payments!"
"You can't have too many credit cards!"
"Just charge it - you deserve a vacation getaway!"

Soon they were juggling balances from one credit card to the next. Then they refinanced their home to pay off all those credit cards (19 of them to be exact). Interestingly enough, they still received plenty of offers for new credit cards.

Then the bank readjusted the interest rate on that new mortgage, and a new cycle began.

"Here's a new card - free interest for a month!"
"Zero interest, no payments for 90 days!" That got them a new truck - and a new monthly payment.
So they refinanced the house again. Imagine a house with a current market value of $150,000 and a total mortgage of $175,000 and you've got the picture.

The news hit them like a ton of bricks. Brett was being transferred - across the country. They'd have to sell the house. **So what do you do with 21 active credit cards and a mortgage debt like that?**

Brett and Mindy sat in the bankruptcy attorney's office, heads in their hands. "How did we ever get here?", she moaned. The attorney looked back at them across the desk. "Easy enough, really. **You listened to the wrong advice; you followed the wrong path.** You need to really think about where you're going from here."

*"They've put themselves on a **fast downhill slide to destruction,** but not before they recruit a crowd of mixed-up followers who can't tell right from wrong. They give the way of truth a bad name. **They're only out for themselves. They'll say anything, anything, that sounds good to exploit you."***

* * * * * * * * * *

One second he was on a nice smooth downhill slide. The next he was riding a giant wave of snow moving faster and faster, totally out of control. Fighting to stay on top of what felt like a moving mountain (an accurate description), Curt fought back panic as he struggled to keep both skis under himself. *What if I slam into a tree? Worse yet, what if I go over a cliff? Get smashed into the side of a mountain?* The "what if's" ran through his mind over and over.

In a split second everything changed as the avalanche raced over a....cliff. His screams were lost in the roar of snow, ice, and debris as he flew over, catching more "air" than he ever dreamed possible.

Curt woke up in a strange place. Everything was white, and he could see sunlight shining through a wall of...snow! He felt his arms and legs, fingers and toes. Yep, he could move them all. What luck!

Curt dug upward and out of his little snow cave to find himself in very unfamiliar terrain. The words of his skiing buddy came back to mind. **"Curt, buddy, it's OK. It's just on the edge of the off-limits zone.** It'll be all right, and there's an awesome slope right along the edge. You'll catch some great air there. Try it out!" *I caught some air all right. Just great. Now where am I?*

Curt knew they'd be looking for him. He felt around in his pockets for the emergency transponder and flipped the switch on. Grabbing a handful of snow and an energy bar, he thanked God for the back country survival class he'd attended just last month.

As he waited for the search and rescue team, Curt thought about how quickly skiing "on the edge" had turned into skiing "over the edge".

* * * * * * * * * *

*"They've put themselves on a **fast downhill slide to destruction,**....God knows how to rescue the godly from evil trials."*

Which of these true stories catches your attention? How easy it is, especially when our lives are busy and seem to move faster every day, to find ourselves "over the edge", following who-knows-what, sliding who-knows-where!

The Good News is that we can change course with God's help. God truly does know how to rescue those who strive to follow Christ more and more closely. God knows we make mistakes, and God desires more than anything else to teach us to recognize and avoid the "false teachers and prophets" in our lives.

God has a powerful "search and rescue team", headed up by our Lord and Savior, Jesus the Christ. You can access it by turning on your emergency transponder - it's called prayer. Tune yourself to the "God-frequency". **The Jesus Rescue Team** (Jesus and His followers) will help you readjust your focus and priorities (away from the earthly and toward the heavenly), motivate and guide you to good stewardship of your earthly (and heavenly) resources, and keep you out of the "off-limits" zones too - if you'll just call, stay in conversation, and build a strong relationship with Him.

Wouldn't you rather be on His "uphill slide" (toward heaven) than on the "downhill slide" toward (well...)?

Reflections

Which "downhill slide" story to you best relate to? Why do you think this is?

Can you think of other examples of life's "downhill slides"? Describe one.

What, in your own words, is the difference between an "uphill slide" and a "downhill slide" as defined in these examples?

32

Return to Sender

God is especially incensed against these "teachers" who live by lust, addicted to a filthy existence. They despise interference from true authority, preferring to indulge in self-rule. Insolent egotists, they don't hesitate to speak evil against the most splendid of creatures. Even angels, their superiors in every way, wouldn't think of throwing their weight around like that, trying to slander others before God. These people are nothing but brute beasts, born in the wild, predators on the prowl. In the very act of bringing down others with their ignorant blasphemies, they themselves will be brought down, losers in the end.

Their evil will boomerang on them. They're so despicable and addicted to pleasure that they indulge in wild parties, carousing in broad daylight. They're obsessed with adultery, compulsive in sin, seducing every vulnerable soul they come upon. Their specialty is greed, and they're experts at it. Dead souls! They've left the main road and are directionless, having taken the way of Balaam, son of Beor, the prophet who turned profiteer, a connoisseur of evil. But Balaam was stopped in his wayward tracks: A dumb animal spoke in a human voice and prevented the prophet's craziness.

There's nothing to these people--they're dried-up fountains, storm-scattered clouds, headed for a black hole in hell. They are loudmouths, full of hot air, but still they're dangerous. Men and women who have recently escaped from a deviant life are most susceptible to their brand of seduction. They promise these newcomers freedom, but they themselves are slaves of corruption, for if they're addicted to corruption--and they are--they're enslaved.

If they've escaped from the slum of sin by experiencing our Master and Savior, Jesus Christ, and then slid back into that same old life again, they're worse than if they had never left. Better not to have started out on the straight road to God than to start out and then turn back, repudiating the experience and the holy command. They prove the point of the proverbs, "A dog goes back to its own vomit," and, "A scrubbed-up pig heads for the mud."

- 2 Peter 2: 10-22 (The Message Version)

* * * * * * * * * *

We sang. We prayed. Sang again. Then we all sat, waiting expectantly for the next part of the worship. Some looked around. Some began to readjust clothing, move coats. A woman on the aisle got up to leave, whispering something to her companion about using the restroom. The voice stopped all that.

First we heard a chord of soft music, then the voice sang.
"She is running...a hundred miles an hour, in the wrong direction.
She is trying...but the canyon's ever widening, in the depths of her cold heart.

109

So she sets out on another misadventure just to find -
She's another two years older, and she's three more steps behind..."

The singer sat on the chair (I hadn't even noticed that chair), cradling her guitar in her lap, **and began to speak.**

"Anybody here like her? Anybody here start out on the straight road with Jesus, only to get lost? Anybody here turn back? Anybody here living with a whole bunch of trash that's sort of bounced back into your life like that boomerang Scripture just talked about?"

I looked up at the close-up video monitor above us. **Tears glistened in her eyes** and blurred her voice as she once again began to sing.

"She is yearning...for shelter and affection - that she never found at home.
She is searching...for a hero to ride in - to ride in and save the day.
And in walks her Prince Charming - and he knows just what to say.
Momentary lapse of reason - and she gives herself away."

She laid the guitar back in her lap as the last word echoed through the church.
"Anybody here ever yearn for something? Something good? Anybody here ever search? I mean, really search, like your life depended on it?" She looked up, meeting eyes as she looked at us.

"My name's Maria. Glad to meet you. So, **anybody here ever met their Prince Charming?** Princess Charming?" (some laughter at this adjustment) "I'm serious now. Anybody ever give it all away, only to find out what you got was nothing - or worse?"

Maria reached over and picked up the Bible from the Communion table. Opening it, she shook her head. "Wow. Let's see. Any of those charming people turn out like this: '...*who live by lust, addicted to a filthy existence. They despise interference from true authority, preferring to indulge in self-rule. Insolent egotists, they don't hesitate to speak evil against the most splendid of creatures. Even angels, their superiors in every way, wouldn't think of throwing their weight around like that, trying to slander others before God.'? How about this: "Their specialty is greed, and they're experts at it...There's nothing to these people--they're dried-up fountains,...'?"*

She looked up, and I could swear she looked right at me. Maybe through me would be a better description. Then she read again: "'*Better **not to have started out on the straight road to God than to start out and then turn back, repudiating the experience and the holy command.**'" That about how you felt when you realized where you'd ended up? Ever think there was no hope - that **God couldn't possibly want you back?**"

"Well, if that's you, then I have another Word for you."
She flipped through some pages, nodded in satisfaction, and began to read once more. *"By this time a lot of men and women of doubtful reputation were hanging around Jesus, listening intently. The Pharisees and religion scholars were not pleased, not at all pleased. They growled, 'He takes in sinners and eats meals with them, treating them like old friends.' (Luke 15:1-2 - The Message Version)*

Their grumbling triggered this story. **"Suppose one of you had a hundred sheep and lost one.** *Wouldn't you leave the ninety-nine in the wilderness and go after the lost one until you found it? When found, you can be sure you would put it across your shoulders, rejoicing, and when you got home call in your friends and neighbors, saying, 'Celebrate with me! I've found my lost sheep!' Count on it--there's more joy in heaven over one sinner's rescued life than over ninety-nine good people in no need of rescue." (Luke 15:3-7 - The Message Version)*

Maria closed the Bible, carefully placing it back on the Communion Table. She looked down as if in prayer. When Maria looked back up, we could see tears running down her face.

"My friends, I have three words for you: Return to Sender. That's right. It may not be easy, but it's worth it. Return to your Sender. Today. Right now."

She began to pick her guitar up again, then changed her mind. **"Oh, and one more thing.** Please hear what I'm about to share with you. We're all here to BE the Body of Christ. You know, the here-and-now hands, feet, and voice of that Shepherd I just read about. To help each other return to our Sender, our Creator. **Return - to - Sender."**

Maria picked up her guitar and began to sing once more.
"Does anybody hear her? Can anybody see?
Or does anybody even know she's going down today?
Under the shadow of our steeple - with all the lost and lonely people?
Searching for the hope that's tucked away in you and me?
Does anybody hear her? Can anybody see?
If judgment looms under every steeple...
And lofty glances from lofty people....
Can't see past her scarlet letter....
and they haven't even met her."

She stood up slowly as the last note soaked through us. Maria walked out the side door in the front of the church. Not a sound - nothing. Over two hundred people sat still and quiet as her words resonated in minds and hearts.

As soft music began to play, **these words appeared on the video screens: "Return to Sender".**
The rest of the worship was changed in that instant. Music continued as we were invited to a time of prayer, a time to consider where we were on the journey with Jesus, a time to pray about our sisters and brothers, a time to pray for open eyes, ears, and hearts.

Return to Sender.

* * * * * * * * * *

Most of us could describe ourselves in various ways. In some ways, we're on the road with Christ. In other ways, we're lost. Perhaps we've followed some 'charming' people in our lives. Maybe we're there now, asking ourselves, "What now?". The road back to our Sender, our Creator, seems longer and harder than it ever seemed before.

Maria's right, you know. Return to your Sender, because He's the Shepherd of your soul. He's searching. He's yearning. For you. Take your lost-ness, your mistake-recovery needs - to Him.
Return. His grace and love will give you the strength and direction you need.

Reflections

In what ways are you "on the road with Christ"? In what ways are you "lost"?

We all have "lost" times and places in our lives. How would you counsel a friend about taking the "lost" parts of their life and "Returning them to the Sender"?

33

Loss Prevention

*This is my second letter to you, dear friends, and in both of them **I have tried to stimulate your wholesome thinking and refresh your memory. I want you to remember what the holy prophets said long ago and what our Lord and Savior commanded through your apostles.***

*Most importantly, **I want to remind you that in the last days scoffers will come, mocking the truth and following their own desires.** They will say, "What happened to the promise that Jesus is coming again? From before the times of our ancestors, everything has remained the same since the world was first created."*

***They deliberately forget** that God made the heavens by the word of his command, and he brought the earth out from the water and surrounded it with water. Then he used the water to destroy the ancient world with a mighty flood. And by the same word, the present heavens and earth have been stored up for fire. They are being kept for the day of judgment, when ungodly people will be destroyed.*

But you must not forget this one thing, dear friends:** A day is like a thousand years to the Lord, and a thousand years is like a day. The Lord isn't really being slow about his promise, as some people think. No, **he is being patient for your sake. He does not want anyone to be destroyed, but wants everyone to repent.

But the day of the Lord will come as unexpectedly as a thief.** Then the heavens will pass away with a terrible noise, and the very elements themselves will disappear in fire, and the earth and everything on it will be found to deserve judgment. Since everything around us is going to be destroyed like this, what holy and godly lives you should live, looking forward to the day of God and hurrying it along. On that day, he will set the heavens on fire, and the elements will melt away in the flames. But **we are looking forward to the new heavens and new earth he has promised, a world filled with God's righteousness. *- 2 Peter 3: 1-13 (New Living Translation)*

* * * * * * * * * *

"I want to tell you about my new job, but it's not really the actual job...well, maybe it IS the REAL job." This was an interesting response to the pastor's invitation for people in the congregation to tell of ways God was working in their lives during the past week.

Amy, a young adult new to the congregation (and church in general) almost sat down when she saw Pastor Jerry's puzzled expression. But then he smiled with encouragement, so she settled in front of the microphone and began her story.

"Yeah, well, I started this new job a couple of weeks ago. 'Loss Prevention', they call it. What I found out is, it means keeping people from stealing stuff. I've learned a lot about people these last two weeks, but I'd say I've learned the most about myself. The latest thing was when I **caught this boy trying to steal some sandwiches.** He didn't really steal them. I mean, I caught him before he got out of the store. I asked him why he needed to steal sandwiches; I mean, why not a DVD, or something cool like other kids were always trying to take? **Turns out his mom and dad had left.** This eleven-year-old boy was now trying to feed his little five-year-old twin brother and sister. They lived in the apartments next to the store."

Amy paused as a few in the congregation gasped, and many more looked shocked.

"Yeah, **so I decided to buy them some food,** including the sandwiches. We called social services too, so those kids could get some real help, but until then I got them some food. Checked up on them on my break that day too. **Do you know I've never stopped being criticized about helping that boy.** 'Just a little thief', 'future delinquent', and 'So, you gonna help every little shoplifter that comes in here - you won't have any paycheck left!' were just some of the nicer things my coworkers said to me."

"So, as I was praying the other night, it came to me. **Loss Prevention. It really IS my job**. Not just at work, either. **I found myself backing off helping** that boy. I found myself listening to those coworker voices. **Then I realized the most important 'Loss Prevention' of all.** It's not about sandwiches, DVDs, or whatever; it's about preventing the loss of my life in Christ. That's right, **it's about eternal Loss Prevention."**

"So I'm here today to share what I learned and to ask you a question, because **it's not just me** who faces forces that will weaken and steal my faith. It's all of us. Here it is. **How's your Loss Prevention coming?"**

The entire congregation was silent as Amy returned to her seat.

* * * * * * * * * *

That's what Peter is addressing when he tells the people this:
"I have tried to stimulate your wholesome thinking and refresh your memory. I want you to remember what the holy prophets said long ago and what our Lord and Savior commanded through your apostles.

Most importantly, I want to remind you that in the last days scoffers will come, mocking the truth and following their own desires. ...They deliberately forget ..."

Peter is warning them about the forces in the world that will seek to damage and destroy their faith and life of discipleship with Jesus the Christ. He is giving them a 'reality check' about living as genuine, practicing Christians in the real world. Peter is indeed encouraging them (and us) to practice spiritual 'Loss Prevention'.

After warning them and teaching about the realities of living faithful lives, Peter gives them an ultimate encouragement. He tells them **the one thing they are not to forget:**

*"But you must not forget this one thing, dear friends: A day is like a thousand years to the Lord, and a thousand years is like a day. The Lord isn't really being slow about his promise, as some people think. No, **he is being patient for your sake. He does not want anyone to be destroyed, but wants everyone to repent."***

So he's saying that **the struggles in the world are real.** The eternal battle is real. **Most importantly he wants them - and us - to know that God is with us.** When we make mistakes, when we suffer losses in our faith and find ourselves walking further and further away from Jesus as our Lord and Savior, we can and must turn back. **We must practice faithful Loss Prevention.**

Can you feel it? Can you see it? God is rooting for you! In the eternal battle for your soul, your very being, God is always patient. **God is King of the Loss Prevention department, where we are all called to serve in our uniquely created ways.**
Let's get to work!

Reflections

In your own words, what is spiritual "loss prevention"?

Why do you think Amy felt herself "backing off" helping the boy?

How do we deal with times when we're in similar situations?

What does it look like to practice "faithful loss prevention"?

34

Twist and Spin

Therefore, beloved, while you are waiting for these things, strive to be found by him at peace, without spot or blemish; and regard the patience of our Lord as salvation. **So also our beloved brother Paul wrote to you according to the wisdom given him,** *speaking of this as he does in all his letters.*

There are some things in them hard to understand, **which the ignorant and unstable twist to their own destruction, as they do the other scriptures.** *You therefore, beloved, since you are forewarned, beware that you are not carried away with the error of the lawless and lose your own stability.*

But grow in the grace and knowledge of our Lord and Savior Jesus Christ. To him be the glory both now and to the day of eternity. Amen.

- 2 Peter 3: 14-18 (New Revised Standard Version)

So, my dear friends, since this is what you have to look forward to, do your very best to be found living at your best, in purity and peace. Interpret our Master's patient restraint for what it is: salvation. **Our good brother Paul, who was given much wisdom in these matters, refers to this in all his letters, and has written you essentially the same thing.**

Some things Paul writes are difficult to understand. **Irresponsible people who don't know what they are talking about twist them every which way.** *They do it to the rest of the Scriptures, too, destroying themselves as they do it. But you, friends, are well-warned. Be on guard lest you lose your footing and get swept off your feet by these lawless and loose-talking teachers.*

Grow in grace and understanding of our Master and Savior, Jesus Christ.

-2 Peter 3: 14-18 (The Message Version)

* * * * * * * * * *

As members of the small group shared how the week had been for them, Brett, new to the group, spoke up. "Remember when we were kids, how we used to sit in a swing and twist it around and around and around?

And then...then let go..and spin! Well, that's how my life has been, and I just have one question. When does the spinning stop? I mean, **I've got my life so completely twisted up and, well, things have all just let loose. I'm spinning so fast, and I'm so darn dizzy that lately I have no clue where I am or where I'm going!"**

Chin-Hui, who had been a part of the "Prayer and Share" group for almost a year now, smiled. "Oh yeah," he nodded, "I remember that. **It really helped me to know that the swing I was twisting and spinning in was never out of God's embrace, never apart from God's grace.** I know that might seem lame to you right now; it seemed that way to me when someone told me that a year ago too. But now, well,...OK. It's Brett, right?"

Brett nodded, and Chin-Hui continued. **"Have you ever swung - clear and straight and high?** Ever felt the wind in your hair, blowing past your face? Well, my new friend, that's like grace blowing through your life. Pretty soon, when the spinning stops and you're all unwound from the junk in your life (with God's help), kick out straight and strong into your new life in Christ. **My brother, you'll know grace like you've never dreamed it could be.** Oh, and one other thing. We're all here to show Jesus to each other - all the time. **So if you ever think there's no grace around you, just call one of us. Deal?"**

Brett smiled - for the first time that day. "Deal", he sighed.

That was the beginning of the end of Brett's 'twist and spin' way of life, as he so fondly called it. He went on to become an AmeriCorps Habitat for Humanity construction supervisor, helping families who, like himself, had found themselves caught up in life's 'twist and spin'. He helped guide them to the clear and straight life path of Christ. He helped them discover and experience God's grace blowing through their lives.

Brett showed them how to, *"Grow in grace and understanding of our Master and Savior, Jesus Christ."*

✻ ✻ ✻ ✻ ✻ ✻ ✻ ✻ ✻

Even if you are twisting or spinning (and most of us are in some area), there is great strength, comfort, and healing in knowing that God never, ever lets us go. We can never, ever be outside God's grace.
As you think about the "twists" going on in your life, hear these words of Scripture and let them echo through those areas of your life as you witness God's awesome power to transform you:

The Lord is my shepherd; I have all that I need. He lets me rest in green meadows; he leads me beside peaceful streams. He renews my strength. He guides me along right paths, bringing honor to his name. Even when I walk through the darkest valley, I will not be afraid, for you are close beside me. Your rod and your staff protect and comfort me. You prepare a feast for me in the presence of my enemies. You honor me by anointing my head with oil. My cup overflows with blessings. Surely your goodness and unfailing love will pursue me all the days of my life, and I will live in the house of the Lord forever.
- Psalm 23:1-6 (New Living Translation)

Then Jesus said, "Come to me, all of you who are weary and carry heavy burdens, and I will give you rest. Take my yoke upon you. Let me teach you, because I am humble and gentle at heart, and you will find rest for your souls. For my yoke is easy to bear, and the burden I give you is light."
- Matthew 11:28-30 (New Living Translation)

Reflections

How have you let the world twist what you know is good and right and godly, until it looks like something else completely?

How have you stood as an agent of the 'straight, clear, grace-powered' life in your world?

Think of areas in your life where you could honestly say you are 'twisting and spinning' right now. Are you inviting God into those areas? Are you spending time with God, allowing God's grace to empower you, God's strong Presence to help untwist those places?

If areas of your life are spinning out of control (or if you have a friend or loved one to whom this applies), are you talking to God about it? Are you seeking the grace of Christ to calm the spin, to set you (or them) on that clear, straight path of grace?

First John

35

Light-Soaked

We declare to you what was from the beginning, what we have heard, what we have seen with our eyes, what we have looked at and touched with our hands, concerning the word of life-- this life was revealed, and we have seen it and testify to it, and declare to you the eternal life that was with the Father and was revealed to us-- we declare to you what we have seen and heard so that you also may have fellowship with us; and truly our fellowship is with the Father and with his Son Jesus Christ.

We are writing these things so that our joy may be complete. This is the message we have heard from him and proclaim to you, that **God is light and in him there is no darkness at all.** If we say that we have fellowship with him while we are walking in darkness, we lie and do not do what is true; but **if we walk in the light as he himself is in the light, we have fellowship with one another, and the blood of Jesus his Son cleanses us from all sin.**

If we say that we have no sin, we deceive ourselves, and the truth is not in us. **If we confess our sins, he who is faithful and just will forgive us our sins and cleanse us from all unrighteousness.** If we say that we have not sinned, we make him a liar, and his word is not in us.   - 1 John 1 (New Revised Standard Version)

From the very first day, we were there, taking it all in--we heard it with our own ears, saw it with our own eyes, verified it with our own hands. The Word of Life appeared right before our eyes; we saw it happen! And now we're telling you in most sober prose that what we witnessed was, incredibly, this: The infinite Life of God himself took shape before us. We saw it, we heard it, and now we're telling you so you can experience it along with us, this experience of communion with the Father and his Son, Jesus Christ.

Our motive for writing is simply this: We want you to enjoy this, too. Your joy will double our joy! This, in essence, is the message we heard from Christ and are passing on to you: **God is light, pure light; there's not a trace of darkness in him.** If we claim that we experience a shared life with him and continue to stumble around in the dark, we're obviously lying through our teeth--we're not living what we claim. But **if we walk in the light, God himself being the light, we also experience a shared life with one another, as the sacrificed blood of Jesus, God's Son, purges all our sin.**

If we claim that we're free of sin, we're only fooling ourselves. A claim like that is errant nonsense. On the other hand, **if we admit our sins--make a clean breast of them--he won't let us down; he'll be true to himself. He'll forgive our sins and purge us of all wrongdoing.** If we claim that we've never sinned, we out-and-out contradict God--make a liar out of him. A claim like that only shows off our ignorance of God.

   - 1 John 1 (The Message Version)

* * * * * * * * *

Adventure. **Adventure! ADVENTURE!!**   That was the group's attitude at the beginning of the **"really cool cave tour"** their friend Jay had promised. Of course when the time came to actually go, he was busy. Jay had, however, given them a "really good map" with directions and "cool things you gotta see" marked on it.

They had followed the map very carefully, but...... Maybe they had taken a wrong turn. Maybe....just maybe there was a wrong turn marked on the map. **Anyway, they got lost.**
It had taken the three explorers a while to figure out just how lost they really were. Now, after an hour or more of wandering around trying to retrace their steps and turns, they had no clue where they were. **Their flashlights had been slowly getting dimmer** until now only two had any power at all. A minute later Lon's light went out. OK, one light left. Molly decided to go explore the path to the right. It 'felt right' to her. Go figure....

"How did we ever let Jay talk us into this?" Zandi stopped and groaned as she leaned back against the cave wall. She could barely see Lon as he shook his head. "Yeah, and what made us try this without him? **Now what are we going to do?"**

Just then they heard Molly's footsteps coming closer. "Hey guys, the path that way climbs up. Let's try it - what do you think?" Zandi rolled her eyes (good thing Molly couldn't see her). "But Molly, we've tried a bunch of climbing in here, and it always leads to a dead end. Why should this one be any different?"

Molly shone the remaining flashlight beam at her own face. "Because....**I think there's light coming from somewhere up that path!"** Zandi and Lon scrambled to their feet. Lon spoke first. "Well, why didn't you say so?" Zandi brushed her jeans off. "OK Molly, let's go!"

Sure enough, the light grew and grew as they hiked out of the cave system. That night they pitched tents and set up camp. As the three friends gathered around the campfire, they talked about what it was like in the pitch black of the cave. Lon grinned across the glow of the fire. "Yeah, Molly, you left with the only light. **We were stuck in the dark, and I've never been in dark that was so.... well, so DARK!"** He almost thought Zandi didn't hear him until she responded. **"You know, we had light down there. We had each other. We were the light.** You know, you could go crazy down there alone in the dark. You could die down there and they might never find you. Ever."

Molly laughed. "Yeah, and **you should have seen your faces when I came back** and told you about that light coming in down the pathway. I could tell you weren't sure...." They started to deny it. She laughed again. "I'm not putting you down. I'd have been the same way. Funny thing, when I was going along that path in the dark, before I saw that little glimmer of light, I got real scared. I thought how I was all alone. I could get lost in there and no one would ever find me. I mean, I went around three or four turns, and in the dark you'd never have found me..."

Always the serious one of the group, Zandi looked deep into the campfire flames. **"We had to accept that light.** The one in each other and the one you found, Molly. We had to be willing to believe it and follow it. **Not so different than life, really."**

Lon looked up into her eyes. "Remember when I first asked you about the 'God thing'? It was right after my dad died, then my mom four months later. **Talk about living in the dark....** You know, you guys were light for me then. **I sure wish Jay had come today.** I think I know why he didn't. You probably don't know, but Sarah broke up with him last night - just when he'd bought a ring and everything. I tried to call him right before I left to meet you, but..... I think you're right, Zandi. **He's got to be willing to believe and accept the light we can be for him.** I really hope he does."

* * * * * * * * * *

"God is light, and in Him there is no darkness at all." Sounds great, doesn't it (well, unless there are some things we'd rather God didn't see)? But as we read along, we see that we have a choice. *"...if we walk in the light as He Himself is in the light, we have fellowship with one another..."*

Ah, so **fellowship with each other concentrates the Light of Christ!** We can (and should) be that holy Light for each other.

And **what about those things we'd rather God didn't see** - those things we'd rather leave in the complete darkness? Well....listen again: *"...if we admit our sins - make a clean breast of them -* **He won't let us down;** *He'll be true to Himself. He'll forgive our sins and purge us of all wrongdoing."* Wow!

So here's the question: will we choose (yes, choose) to be soaked in His Light, or will we let that Light stay a tiny glimmer? I don't know about you, but *"stumbling around in the dark"* doesn't seem too attractive to me.

As we increase our time spent sharing with other Christ-followers, the light in each of our lives will grow until we can each feel the power of that holy Light soaking our spirits to the very core.
We'll indeed be....Light-soaked!

Reflections

How would you respond to Zandi's statements when she said:
"You know, we had light down there. We had each other. We were the light."

"We had to accept that light. The one in each other and the one you found, Molly. We had to be willing to believe it and follow it. **Not so different than life, really."**

Lon is grieving for his friend Jay.
What do you think he can do to follow up his statement that, "He's got to be willing to believe and accept the light we can be for him."?

36

In...or Out?

My little children, I am writing these things to you so that you may not sin. **But if anyone does sin, we have an advocate with the Father, Jesus Christ the righteous;** *and he is the atoning sacrifice for our sins, and not for ours only but also for the sins of the whole world.*

Now by this we may be sure that we know him, if we obey his commandments. **Whoever says, "I have come to know him," but does not obey his commandments, is a liar,** *and in such a person the truth does not exist; but whoever obeys his word, truly in this person the love of God has reached perfection. By this we may be sure that we are in him:* **whoever says, "I abide in him," ought to walk just as he walked.**

- 1 John 2: 1-6 (New Revised Standard Version)

I write this, dear children, to guide you out of sin. **But if anyone does sin, we have a Priest-Friend in the presence of the Father: Jesus Christ, righteous Jesus.** *When he served as a sacrifice for our sins, he solved the sin problem for good--not only ours, but the whole world's.*

Here's how we can be sure that we know God in the right way: Keep his commandments. If **someone claims, "I know him well!" but doesn't keep his commandments, he's obviously a liar.** *His life doesn't match his words. But the one who keeps God's word is the person in whom we see God's mature love. This is the only way to be sure we're in God.* **Anyone who claims to be intimate with God ought to live the same kind of life Jesus lived.**

- 1 John 2: 1-6 (The Message Version)

* * * * * * * * * *

The stakes were high. Many of the guys on the varsity baseball team were seniors. In this last year of their high school sports careers, several were hoping for college baseball scholarships. Adding to the excitement, the team was good enough to make their division playoffs, and maybe, just maybe take the championship for the first time in over thirty years!

 As Bert stood with some of the guys on the team outside the gym, center fielder Andy challenged him. **"So Bert, are you in or are you out?"**

The group stood around - just waiting for his answer. Bert remembered feeling really cool telling the guys he'd join their little plan, but now....after some thought, he'd realized that this could be dangerous. **What would his mom say if he got hurt?**

Andy got closer to Bert and spoke a little louder. **"Well? If you're not in - all the way in - you need to leave.** We've got plans to make. So...?" Bert's mind scrambled. Those "other guys" lived on his street, and he had a little sister. What if....?

Micah spoke up. **"Bert, I bet I know what you're thinking.** Remember, the first disciples had those 'other guys' on their streets, in their neighborhoods too. I bet some were even in their families. They had to decide, and you do too. **Are you walking with Jesus today, or not? You can't walk halfway with Him, you know."**

Ed, silent until now, moved so he was right in front of Bert. **"You know buddy, what they're doing isn't right.** Just because somebody talks different, dresses different, and acts different, that doesn't mean God loves them any less. Christ came for them too, died for them too. You know that. So what's the problem?"

"Well, I guess it really isn't right. I mean, Kai and Jin, they have awesome throwing arms, and can they ever hit the ball! And that Tiwo, I bet his fastball hits 90. **Why didn't they make the team?** I mean, the coaches didn't even hardly ask them to play!" Bert was still puzzled.

Ed blew the breath out he'd been holding. "OK, I know you're new around here, but **around here 'their kind' never get a second look, let alone even a first glance. Got it?"**

Bert had indeed come from a different kind of neighborhood. He'd been one of only three Anglo kids in his entire class, and he'd never been left out. Bert had played ball since second grade. It hadn't mattered that he'd been different. New to this mostly Anglo neighborhood and school, excluding someone based on how they looked or dressed or <u>anything</u> just wasn't in his experience. **But this plan......he just didn't know about this.**

"Well? I'm not asking again. So?" Andy was laying down the challenge now, and Bert decided to step up. **"OK, you're right. If I call myself Christian,** I really can't do any less, can I?" I'm in."

Micah motioned for them all to sit on the grass in a tight circle. "All right, here it is. **There are eight of us, and we're all rostered to start the season opener. None of us will. None.** I've talked to the junior varsity guys, and seven of them are in too. They won't be able to field a team, no matter how they try. And guess who they'll forfeit the game to?"

Looks of sudden comprehension swept around the circle. Ed was the first to speak. "Oh my gosh, it's absolutely perfect! We'll lose to Northwest - that's your old school, Bert!"

Bert was getting the whole picture now. "You guys know what can happen, right? I don't know about all of you, but **I graduate this year, and I need that baseball scholarship.** What if they throw us all off the team? My mom would kill me!"

Ed, ever the logical one (headed off next year to engineering school) laughed. **"So just who do you think they'll get to play?** I can just see it now. You think those coaches don't know how good Tiwo is? They'd have to be blind. And I know for a fact that Coach Mike was watching that game at the rec center field when Kai and Jin hit those back to back homers. You can't tell me he didn't see that. No way!"

So **those eight guys showed up at the game - in the stands.** The coaches were furious (a mild description). **Coach Mike was chosen by the head coach to talk to the guys,** who told him to either get them to suit up or suspend them from the team. Before he could say a word, though, Ed spoke up. **"Hey Coach Mike, saw you in church Sunday.** You really believe all that stuff? I mean, are you a real follower of Christ? Are you in? Or are you out? I can't live my faith part time - maybe you can, but not me. Sorry, Coach."

Coach Mike looked up into the eyes of eight extremely determined young men. **They were right.** He did remember seeing Tiwo pitch. He did remember watching those balls fly way over the rec center fence off the bats of Jin and Kai. Oh yes, he did. "You know guys, **I'm just the junior coach here.** You're all going to be suspended if you don't suit up. You know that, right?"

Looking up across into the stands on the other side, Bert saw some of his friends from the old neighborhood. It all became clear in that moment, and he spoke up. **"So Coach Mike, how about you?** There's room on this bench for you too. **You a real Christian, or just a part-timer?** Seems like you were just a few seats away from me last Sunday. What was that the preacher said again? Something like...'Anyone who claims they're followers ought to live like it', yep, something like that. **Well? You in - or out?"**

The game was forfeited. Those eight guys (and Coach Mike) were suspended. When the story hit the regional news though, things changed. **The team ended the season with ten wins and one loss** - the forfeited game. The star pitcher? Tiwo. The top hitters? Andy, Micah, Jin, and Kai.

Those young men found great power as they walked their faith together - full time. They were indeed "in" with Jesus. How about us? We're not expected to be perfect, but hear these words of Scripture once more: *"But if anyone does sin, we have a Priest-Friend in the presence of the Father: Jesus Christ, righteous Jesus."*

Hear these words too:
"If someone claims, 'I know him well!' but doesn't keep his commandments, he's obviously a liar. His life doesn't match his words. But the one who keeps God's word is the person in whom we see God's mature love. This is the only way to be sure we're in God. Anyone who claims to be intimate with God ought to live the same kind of life Jesus lived."

Reflections

Who do you "walk together" with as you do your best to live out your faith each day?

What kinds of risks do Christians you know take in their everyday lives to live as Jesus teaches?

John Wesley, considered to be the founder of Methodism, said that we are all "going on to perfection". Considering what you've experienced in this chapter, what does that mean to you?

37

Up Close and Personal

Beloved, I am writing you no new commandment, but an old commandment that you have had from the beginning; the old commandment is the word that you have heard. Yet **I am writing you a new commandment that is true in him and in you,** *because the darkness is passing away and the true light is already shining.*

Whoever says, "I am in the light," while hating a brother or sister, is still in the darkness. **Whoever loves a brother or sister lives in the light,** *and in such a person there is no cause for stumbling. But whoever hates another believer is in the darkness, walks in the darkness, and does not know the way to go, because the darkness has brought on blindness.*

I am writing to you, little children, because **your sins are forgiven on account of his name.** *I am writing to you, fathers, because* **you know him who is from the beginning.** *I am writing to you, young people, because* **you have conquered the evil one.** *I write to you, children, because* **you know** *the Father. I write to you, fathers, because* **you know** *him who is from the beginning. I write to you, young people, because* **you are strong and the word of God abides in you, and you have overcome the evil one.** *-1 John 2:7-14 (New Revised Standard Version)*

My dear friends, I'm not writing anything new here. This is the oldest commandment in the book, and you've known it from day one. It's always been implicit in the Message you've heard. On the other hand, perhaps **it is new, freshly minted as it is in both Christ and you**--*the darkness on its way out and the True Light already blazing!*

Anyone who claims to live in God's light and hates a brother or sister is still in the dark. **It's the person who loves brother and sister who dwells in God's light and doesn't block the light from others.** *But whoever hates is still in the dark, stumbles around in the dark, doesn't know which end is up, blinded by the darkness.*

I remind you, my dear children: **Your sins are forgiven in Jesus' name.** *You veterans were in on the ground floor, and* **know the One** *who started all this; you newcomers have* **won a big victory over the Evil One.** *And a second reminder, dear children:* **You know the Father from personal experience.** *You veterans* **know the One who started it all**; *and you newcomers--***such vitality and strength! God's word is so steady in you. Your fellowship with God enables you to gain a victory over the Evil One.** *- 1 John 2:7-14 (The Message Version)*

* * * * * * * * *

"You know, when his friend told me about him - how great he was, how good looking, how much fun, how caring....well, that was good. In fact it all turned out to be true, but now, well, now..." She blushed, and reached down for her napkin on the table as tears filled her eyes.

Sue raised her glass again to toast her sweetheart. "Twenty years. Today." All eyes were watching her as she continued. **"Things happen,** you know? Things. Like losing jobs - and gaining triplets - at the same time. Things like floods that take away everything you thought you had. Things like birthdays and new starts. **You learn how close 'close' really is.** You learn that evil and wrong really do exist - and they do have power. And you learn that **God is as up close and personal - and as powerful - as you let God be in your life."**

She turned and winked at her husband Bo seated next to her. **"We've got each other. We've got all of you, and we've got God - up close and personal."**

Bo stood as Sue sat down. "Well, since we're getting 'up close and personal'..." He bent down and whispered in her ear, and Sue blushed and chuckled as she tried to keep from choking on her champagne.

"So, since we're getting personal here, right over there is that 'friend' Sue just mentioned. Hey Tad, stand up and take a bow." Now it was Tad's turn to almost choke. He knew Bo well, and the look on Bo's face told him he was definitely up to something...

"So, I'm good looking, fun, and caring, huh? Well, here's what my good buddy Tad told me about my beautiful, fun, and caring wife: nothing! He just grinned when I asked him. You know that grin he gets..." Soft laughter rippled through the crowd.

Bo picked up his glass and lifted it in a toast to Sue, his wife of twenty years. **"Seriously though, we do have God up close and personal.** Sue's right - we've lost jobs and gained triplets, had floods and new starts - those things have tested us. But through it all, **Christ is new every day.** He never, ever leaves us. In fact, I see Him fresh each day - in Sue. She's the best up close and personal gift God ever put in my life. So, to Sue, and to twenty more 'up close and personal' years together!"

The sound of applause, cheers, and clinking glasses filled the room as Bo sat down. This time it was Sue's turn to whisper in his ear - and his turn to blush and sputter!

* * * * * * * * *

In this 'hurry-up' world, **sometimes we forget just how 'up close and personal' God is ready to be to us.** We forget just how much God gave to show us the amazing power of our Savior, who is the Way, the Truth, and the Life. We forget what a difference a truly 'up close and personal' relationship with Christ can mean in our lives.

We go on as if we have all the strength, all the power, and all the wisdom we could ever need - all on our own. **Until.** Until the floods, the lost jobs, lost friends, unexplainable calamities overrun us and our well-laid plans. Until something happens and we begin to wonder: **Is this all there is? Why am I here anyway?** Questions and situations come that make us stop and take stock of what's truly important, what powers and empowers us, where we're headed (and why).....**and we wonder.**

If there's nothing/no one on your "up close and personal" list that's forever (beyond your life here on earth) 'up close and personal', I invite you to explore what a relationship with God through Jesus the Christ can mean to you. Talk to a friend whom you know has a close relationship with Christ, or perhaps a pastor in your community. Many times local chaplains or pastors are great conversation partners as you explore the amazing difference knowing Christ (really knowing him - for real) can make in your life.

Above all, don't give up. Look, explore, and ask until you find the answers you need to build an eternally 'up close and personal' relationship with the One who will never, ever leave you. **Christ will give you the strength, wisdom, and comfort you need to ride out any storm life brings your way.** Anything. Anywhere. Forever.

Reflections

What's really 'up close and personal' in our lives? What really matters? What can we really not live meaningfully without? Take a moment to write down your 'up close and personal' list.

Now, is there anything or anyone on your list that lasts forever? Anything or anyone who is so steady, so strong, and so eternal that you'll never lose it or them?

Now stop a moment and think again. If 'God' or 'Jesus' is on your 'up close and personal' list, how up close and personal are you to Him - really? Is He just there for emergency use, or **are you 'up close' each day**?

38

Deep Connections

Do not love this world nor the things it offers you, for when you love the world, you do not have the love of the Father in you. For the world offers only a craving for physical pleasure, a craving for everything we see, and pride in our achievements and possessions. These are not from the Father, but are from this world. And this world is fading away, along with everything that people crave.

*But **anyone who does what pleases God will live forever.** Dear children, the last hour is here. You have heard that the Antichrist is coming, and already many such antichrists have appeared. From this we know that the last hour has come. These people left our churches, but they never really belonged with us; otherwise they would have stayed with us. When they left, it proved that they did not belong with us.*

*But **you are not like that, for the Holy One has given you his Spirit, and all of you know the truth.** So I am writing to you not because you don't know the truth but because **you know the difference between truth and lies.** And who is a liar? Anyone who says that Jesus is not the Christ. Anyone who denies the Father and the Son is an antichrist. Anyone who denies the Son doesn't have the Father, either. But anyone who acknowledges the Son has the Father also.*

*So **you must remain faithful to what you have been taught from the beginning.** If you do, you will remain in fellowship with the Son and with the Father. And **in this fellowship we enjoy the eternal life he promised us.***

- 1 John 2:15-25 (New Living Translation)

* * * * * * * * *

"When I came here, I had no clue why. I mean, I haven't been in a church since I was five years old. That's the year my folks got their divorce and I had to go live with Aunt Tasha. But my friend Mia invited me here. She said it'd be fun, and they'd have free food (the kind I like). And really, who'd miss free chocolate? Not me!" She took a deep breath.

"Anyway, **I figured out that Jesus is really real this weekend.** I learned to see a lot of things for what they really are - lies. And you know what? A lot of people like me, we believe those lies! Pretty soon we're living those lies, and we don't even realize it because it feels so....normal."

She looked at her new friends surrounding her as she stood at the podium. One of them whispered in her ear and handed her a tissue.

"**Oh yeah. I'm Paula, and we're from the table of 'Truth Wins!'**. Anyway, ...'' She dabbed tears from her face as she found her voice again. "Anyway, truth really <u>does</u> win. **People kept telling me that God was testing me, or punishing me, or....something. I sure didn't want to know that Jesus!**''

"So I'm going to go back home and find a church that knows the real Jesus, a place that will help me hold onto Him and learn from Him, a place that will help me grow some deep faith connections. My new friend Ashley says I can come check hers out, but no matter what, **I'm just going to keep learning and living more of the real truth!**''

As Paula stepped to the side, the young women looked at each other to see who'd brave the microphone next. They'd all been on a special retreat, a time away to get closer to God and deepen their lives as followers of Christ, and they'd been invited to share what the retreat had meant to them during the evening's closing worship.

Ashley stepped to the microphone. She took a deep breath, and this time Paula handed her a tissue and laid a hand gently on her shoulder. "OK,'' she began, "It really is almost time to go back home. Home. Well, **I'm going to need His truth where I live.** Right now I'm living in the shelter at the Christian Church down the street from here. **My mom's in jail and my dad, well,** who knows where he is these days. I'm seventeen, and none of those help places want to help me, 'cause I'm too old. **Too old! I always thought, you know, seventy or eighty would be too old for something, but seventeen?** Anyway, I found out I can never be too old, or too young, or too anything for God to love me. Jesus will always want me, and that's the truth. Paula's right. **I've got connections I never even thought about before.** When the world dishes out its lies, I've got forever truth in Jesus. **I'm gonna live in those connections, because they're deeper than any hurt I've ever had,** deeper than any fear I've got, deeper than any mistakes I've made, and deeper than anything I could ever think of. I'm ready!''

As Ashley turned from the microphone, Paula caught her in a strong embrace. Soon all five young women were holding on tightly to each other. As they made the way back to their seats, 'amens' filled the air. This <u>had</u> been <u>some</u> weekend!

* * * * * * * * * *

Many things compete for our attention in today's world. The psychology of advertising is big business. It takes a big faith in a big God to see and live into what is **bedrock truth - Jesus Christ.** Those who claim Jesus as Lord and Savior are called to live in that Truth. We are called to walk in His Way, to live connected to His Life. Way. Truth. Life. **These are the deep connections we claim as disciples of Christ.**

This Scripture speaks of many "antichrists" that have come. Anything that tempts us, pulls us, hooks into our very human temptations and cravings is an "anti-Christ" force in our world. **These things work against the Truth that is Jesus the Christ.** They weaken our faith connections, and sometimes even threaten to destroy them. But God never gives up on us. God wants a deep connection with us. Christ came to point the way for us! As Ashley put it so well, His love-and-grace-filled connections with us are deeper than any fear, any hurt, or any mistakes we've made.

So let's get - and stay - connected. Deeply. Strongly. Forever!

Reflections

What are some things and/or activities that seem to compete with Christ for attention in the wrold today? In your life, that of your family, and friends?

What is the part of Ashley's witness talk that touches you most strongly?

39

Holy Childhood

I am writing to warn you about those people who are misleading you. **But Christ has blessed you with the Holy Spirit.** *Now the Spirit stays in you, and you don't need any teachers. The Spirit is truthful and teaches you everything. So stay one in your heart with Christ, just as the Spirit has taught you to do.*

Children, stay one in your hearts with Christ. *Then when he returns, we will have confidence and won't have to hide in shame. You know that Christ always does right and that* **everyone who does right is a child of God.**

Think how much the Father loves us. **He loves us so much that he lets us be called his children, as we truly are.** *But since the people of this world did not know who Christ is, they don't know who we are. My dear friends,* **we are already God's children,** *though what we will be hasn't yet been seen. But we do know that when Christ returns, we will be like him, because we will see him as he truly is. This hope makes us keep ourselves holy, just as Christ is holy.*
- *1 John 2:26 - 3:3 (Contemporary English Version)*

I've written to warn you about those who are trying to deceive you. But they're **no match for what is embedded deeply within you--Christ's anointing, no less!** *You don't need any of their so-called teaching. Christ's anointing teaches you the truth on everything you need to know about yourself and him, uncontaminated by a single lie. Live deeply in what you were taught.*

And now, **children, stay with Christ. Live deeply in Christ.** *Then we'll be ready for him when he appears, ready to receive him with open arms, with no cause for red-faced guilt or lame excuses when he arrives. Once you're convinced that he is right and righteous, you'll recognize that* **all who practice righteousness are God's true children.**

What marvelous love the Father has extended to us! Just look at it-- **we're called children of God! That's who we really are.** *But that's also why the world doesn't recognize us or take us seriously, because it has no idea who he is or what he's up to. But friends,* **that's exactly who we are: children of God.** *And that's only the beginning. Who knows how we'll end up! What we know is that when Christ is openly revealed, we'll see him--and in seeing him, become like him. All of us who look forward to his Coming stay ready, with the glistening purity of Jesus' life as a model for our own.*
- *1 John 2:26 - 3:3 (The Message Version)*

* * * * * * * * * *

"So how's the 'church thing' going for you, Tim? Haven't seen you in a while."
Tim was a bit surprised to see his old friend Eric in the Christian coffee shop, and his face must have shown it.

He waved at Eric, wondering what brought him here of all places. "Hey Eric, have a seat. Got a minute? I'm buying!"

Eric's broad smile gave him the answer. **"Well, I never turn down a free drink**...even if it is coffee on a Friday night. I just saw your truck and decided to stop to say hi. So, how <u>is</u> the 'church thing' going, anyway?"

Tim stood up. "Let's get you that drink. I could use a refill too. Then **I'll tell you - if you really want to know, that is."** Eric looked at Tim as they waited for their coffee. He seemed different somehow. Hard to put a finger on it, but.... Not really goofy, but certainly happier. Happier in a deeper sort of way. They got their coffee and returned to the table. Tim got that mischievous look Eric knew so well.

Eric paused a minute. "Well....it's weird, but you seem somehow - younger. That's it!" Tim laughed - a relaxed, carefree sound he'd never heard from Tim in the fifteen years they'd been friends. "Well buddy, you've got it! **This 'church thing', as you call it, why, it's like a second childhood."** His face became instantly serious. "I take it back; it's my first childhood. Never thought I'd get anything like this. You ought to try it - really."

Now Eric looked truly uncomfortable. Tim put his cup down, looked at his friend, and waited. Concerned that maybe he'd said something wrong, he shifted gears. "Hey, I didn't mean to shove anything at you. Really. It's just that, well, **if I found a place with the best steak I'd ever eaten**, you'd be the first guy I'd call. This is so much better than that, but we can talk about something else if you want. How's work going?"

Both men drove local delivery trucks for competing companies, so they talked about work for quite a while. Even when they talked about the stress and problems of work, Tim seemed different. More relaxed. Tim had <u>never</u> been relaxed about work! Eric remembered many times when he thought Tim would surely pop a blood vessel venting about the unfair politics and favoritism rampant in his work environment. This change made him more and more curious.

As the conversation paused, Eric changed the subject. **"OK. Tell me how you got a 'second childhood', as you call it. I'm ready."** Tim had his doubts about just how ready Eric was, but OK - he had asked.

"Well, it's about claiming my real self - the one God created. It's about letting myself be one of God's children and letting Him love me no matter what. It's about listening to Jesus as He teaches me how to live that way. Then I just follow His example. Not perfectly of course - that's why we'll always be God's...children. We'll always be learning, till the day we die and meet Him in heaven. Make sense so far?"

Eric laughed (which made Tim worry for a second or two). "Well, you <u>do</u> seem much more excited about this than a good t-bone!" He pointed at Tim's t-shirt. **"When's that men's group thing?"** Tim had forgotten he was even wearing the men's group Habitat for Humanity build shirt. "This weekend. Want to come? The family we're helping build a house for is really great. It's a mom and three little boys. Pick you up around eight?"

Eric didn't even hesitate. "Sure. Do I get a shirt too? And more free coffee? Just kidding. I'll be ready. **I'm interested in learning more about your second childhood...."**

* * * * * * * * *

There's an eternal childhood "embedded deeply within" all of us. No matter how old we get, no matter what life dishes out to us, no matter how "grown up" we are, we are always God's children. His precious children. The world's measure of maturity demands that we be independent, strong, and sure. We are supposed to be happy, confident, and be well into working our (of course self-designed) plan for our lives. **Some of us, like Tim, have never even really had a first childhood.** Some of us had to 'grow up' way too fast. **On the other hand, some seem to have never grown up,** never learned to be responsible for our own choices. These are two extreme responses to the world's demand and definition of 'growing up'. Most of us are somewhere in the middle.

Growing up in faith is different. As we grow closer to God, living as disciples of Christ, we relax more and more into God's arms. As we choose God's way, the way Christ shows us, our choices become more automatically in line with Him. **We mature in faith, but remain forever God's precious children!** We return often to prayer, to Scripture, to sharing with other Christ-followers; we come to God for teaching and nurture in the middle of a world which tempts us with its 'all about you' mentality.

Isn't it good that in the middle of all this, we are firmly claimed as God's children?
Imagine having a childhood that never ends - a holy childhood!

Reflections

How can someone mature, yet remain a child in God's eyes?

What do you think of Tim's statement that, "It's just that, well, if I found a place with the best steak I'd ever eaten, you'd be the first guy I'd call. This is so much better than that,…"

What stops us from thinking (and acting) as Tim did with his friend Eric?

40

Love...Who?

Everyone who commits sin is guilty of lawlessness; sin is lawlessness. You know that he was revealed to take away sins, and in him there is no sin. No one who abides in him sins; no one who sins has either seen him or known him. Little children, let no one deceive you. Everyone who does what is right is righteous, just as he is righteous. Everyone who commits sin is a child of the devil; for the devil has been sinning from the beginning.

The Son of God was revealed for this purpose, to destroy the works of the devil.** Those who have been born of God do not sin, because God's seed abides in them; they cannot sin, because they have been born of God. The children of God and the children of the devil are revealed in this way: **all who do not do what is right are not from God, nor are those who do not love their brothers and sisters.

- *1 John 3:4-10 (New Revised Standard Version)*

Everyone who sins is breaking God's law, for all sin is contrary to the law of God. And you know that Jesus came to take away our sins, and there is no sin in him. Anyone who continues to live in him will not sin. But anyone who keeps on sinning does not know him or understand who he is. Dear children, don't let anyone deceive you about this: When people do what is right, it shows that they are righteous, even as Christ is righteous. But when people keep on sinning, it shows that they belong to the devil, who has been sinning since the beginning.

But the Son of God came to destroy the works of the devil.** Those who have been born into God's family do not make a practice of sinning, because God's life is in them. **So they can't keep on sinning, because they are children of God.** So now we can tell who are children of God and who are children of the devil. **Anyone who does not live righteously and does not love other believers does not belong to God.

- *1 John 3:4-10 (New Living Translation)*

* * * * * * * * *

"But Mo-o-o-o-m! He's weird! Even his toys are....weird! And besides, no one wants to play with him, OK? <u>No one</u>! Why me?" Jordan looked up into the serious, 'you're in trouble now, young man' face of his mom. How could he get out of <u>this</u> one? And, oh my gosh, **what would his friends say** if they saw him with....Casey? I mean, really. **The kid had....dolls!** And weird pasty stuff with even weirder pancake-bread things for lunch. Oh, and then there was that fruit mush he brought to school - way gross!!

"Jordan! **Maybe we're pretty strange to him too, but he's in your class at summer camp**, so he deserves better from you, and remember...."

'**I know, Mom. 'What would Jesus say?' I get it, but still...."**
"No 'buts' about it, young man. Come pack your lunch. We're all going to the zoo together: you, Casey, his mom, and me. And we're going to have a <u>good</u> time."

Feeling assigned to his fate, Jordan tied his shoes (very slowly) and trudged to the kitchen, backpack in hand. Just then, a knock sounded on the back door. Looking through the window, **Jordan saw his neighbor and best friend, Sam. Great! Now he'd be totally humiliated** when the entire neighborhood found out he'd spent the day at the zoo with the weird new kid!

Jordan opened the door and let Sam in. "Hey, what's up?", Sam began. "Where are you guys going?" Jordan thought he might as well get it over with. Blowing out a big sigh, he told Sam, "The zoo, with Casey and his mom..." He waited, looking at Sam, expecting....but wait...**Sam actually looked excited!**

"Hey Jordan, can I come too? Is Casey bringing some of that cool food like he had at church camp? That fruit stuff is awesome! Did you know they have real wild monkeys and tigers where he used to live? Can I come? Please?"

Just then, Jordan's mom came around the corner into the kitchen. "Sure you can come, Sam. Just check with your dad, OK?" Sam was out the door in a flash. Within minutes he was back with an 'OK' note from his dad. "Hey Mrs. Tenney, **I called Casey too, and his mom's making lunch for all of us. Cool, huh?"**

Jordan's mom smiled. Yes, indeed, it was truly 'cool'!

* * * * * * * * * *

So who are our 'brothers and sisters'? Who is this Scripture writer talking about? Do you have any 'Caseys' in your life? You see, **we're actually a lot like Jordan.** We want our 'sisters and brothers' to be a lot like us. We want them to be people we're really comfortable with. We want it to be easy. God rarely seems to work that way though.

God is working hard to transform us, to grow us into fully devoted and connected followers of Christ. The stakes are high, and there are forces in this world that work very hard to thwart and destroy our transformation.

"But the Son of God came to destroy the works of the devil. Those who have been born into God's family do not make a practice of sinning, because God's life is in them. So they can't keep on sinning, because they are children of God."

The 'devil', or the evil forces loose in the world (whatever you call them) **are genuine.**

As we learn to recognize and treat people as Christ would treat them, we join the forces of God's kingdom in the world. We act for and with Christ to transform the world. **We say with our actions, "I'm with Him, and together we're destroying the works of the devil."** We say, "I'm born into God's family, and I do sin sometimes, but when I'm living in Him it's not a habit or a practice with me, because I'm a child of the Light, a child of God."

We have choices every minute of every day. Who and Whose are we? Are we more like Jordan, or more like Sam? When God places someone in our lives (even if it's for a short time), do we show them Christ? Or do we answer God with, "Love...who?"

When we're tempted like Jordan was, let's picture Jesus, our Lord and Savior. Let's picture Him looking down from the cross. How did He answer the 'love...who' question? He answered it with a strong, clear 'I love them - ALL of them' answer - an answer He died and rose again for.

Who will you be called on to love with His love? Who and Whose are you?
Remember that **God loves.....YOU!**

Reflections

Why do you think many people cringe at statements such as, "God loves you...and so do I!"?

Think of a time when you were more like Jordan? Why do you think this was?

Now think of a time when you were more like Sam? Why did you react this way?

Have others ever thought you were "weird", like Casey? If so, how did that feel? Did anyone step up to stand beside you in some way? If so, how did that help you? If not, how did you deal with the situation?

How do (and can) people act with Christ to transform the world?

41

Love Practice Time!

*For **this is the original message we heard: We should love each other.** We must not be like Cain, who joined the Evil One and then killed his brother. And why did he kill him? Because he was deep in the practice of evil, while the acts of his brother were righteous. So don't be surprised, friends, when the world hates you. This has been going on a long time.*

*The way we know we've been transferred from death to life is that we love our brothers and sisters. **Anyone who doesn't love is as good as dead.** Anyone who hates a brother or sister is a murderer, and you know very well that eternal life and murder don't go together.*

__This is how we've come to understand and experience love: Christ sacrificed his life for us.__ This is why we ought to live sacrificially for our fellow believers, and not just be out for ourselves. If you see some brother or sister in need and have the means to do something about it but turn a cold shoulder and do nothing, what happens to God's love? It disappears. And you made it disappear.

__My dear children, let's not just talk about love; let's practice real love. This is the only way we'll know we're living truly, living in God's reality. It's also the way to shut down debilitating self-criticism, even when there is something to it.__ For God is greater than our worried hearts and knows more about us than we do ourselves. We're able to stretch our hands out and receive what we asked for because we're doing what he said, doing what pleases him.

Again, this is God's command: to believe in his personally named Son, Jesus Christ. He told us to love each other, in line with the original command. __As we keep his commands, we live deeply and surely in him, and he lives in us.__ And this is how we experience his deep and abiding presence in us: by the Spirit he gave us.

- 1 John 3:11-24 (The Message Version)

* * * * * * * * * *

"I'm no good. I can't ever get anything right! This is never going to work!!" Carly couldn't help overhearing, even through Leann's almost closed door. Should she knock? What could possibly be so bad?

Carly walked down to the rental truck for the last dolly-load of boxes. Who knew how much work moving into a tiny dorm room could be? Her cousin Joan had come down with her last weekend to measure the room. Then they'd gone back home to measure furniture. Oh yes, and then there was the tiny dorm room closet. Carly figured she'd have just enough space for four outfits for each season - plus one coat and a jacket. Period. She wheeled the last boxes into her room, locked the door, and pushed the empty dolly down the hall.

Again she passed Leann's room. Pausing to read the name plate on the door, yep, "Leann Tilton", she thought she heard crying coming from inside. Carly stopped and gently knocked on the door. She waited. **"Hello? Leann? You OK?"** A faint voice answered, "Come on....in.", so she opened the door slowly.

The sight that greeted her could only be described as chaos. Boxes, lamps, bed, dresser, and loose....stuff, piled in stacks taller than Carly. The voice was coming from somewhere in the middle of all that.

"Leann? Where are you?" She peered around and between the piles, looking for the woman that matched the voice she'd heard. **Just then a box began to topple toward her off the top of one of the stacks.** As Carly caught it, Leann's face appeared where the box had been. She looked clearly upset and overwhelmed.

"Need some help?" Carly asked, not sure where they could even start. It was obvious Leann had about five times more stuff (at least) than would ever fit in that small dorm room! The women looked at each other over the stack of boxes. **Leann was obviously trapped in there.** How had that happened? Carly wondered as she tried to figure out what to say next.

Leann wiped her nose on the back of her sleeve. **"You really want to help?"** Carly nodded, "Sure I do!", and Leann's face relaxed a little.

"Well, here's how it is. **My Mom's got a new boyfriend, and he's got a little girl.** They decided she could have my room, so this morning a delivery truck showed up here with <u>all</u> my stuff. Seems they have a new daughter now." Leann began to cry again.

Carly remembered in that instant how she'd begged (OK, whined) for so many years to her parents for a sister. **Five brothers later, they'd told her six kids was more than enough.** Her next youngest brother had said something really interesting as he'd hugged her goodbye outside the dorms just that morning: "Hey sis, you'll have all kinds of sisters to choose from here!"

Carly looked at Leann and smiled. **"We can do this. That's what new sisters are for!"** A new friendship began that day, and it lasted decades. In fact, they called each other 'best-sister-friends"!

✳ ✳ ✳ ✳ ✳ ✳ ✳ ✳ ✳ ✳

Practicing love. Not just any love - Jesus-love!

Leann was living in the midst of what this Scripture calls 'debilitating self-criticism". Justified? **Carly didn't care - she just loved Leann.** She met her where she was and loved her. Together they had a rummage sale. Together they found storage space for Leann's extra belongings. And when Carly's parents learned that Leann was truly not welcome in her own family, they began to include her in theirs.

Carly truly found the sister she'd always prayed for by practicing love - Jesus-love!

As we begin each day, let's hear Jesus calling us to practice real love - His love. Let's keep inviting Him to live surely and deeply in us as we live in him.

It's love practice time!!

Reflections

What does "love practice time" mean to you after reading this chapter?

What is your response to the Scripture that says, *"My dear children, let's not just talk about love; let's practice real love. This is the only way we'll know we're living truly, living in God's reality. It's also the way to shut down debilitating self-criticism, even when there is something to it. For God is greater than our worried hearts and knows more about us than we do ourselves."*?

42

Origin-al Evidence

*Dear friends, do not believe everyone who claims to speak by the Spirit. You must test them to see if the spirit they have comes from God. For **there are many false prophets in the world.** This is how we know if they have the Spirit of God: If a person claiming to be a prophet acknowledges that Jesus Christ came in a real body, that person has the Spirit of God. But if someone claims to be a prophet and does not acknowledge the truth about Jesus, that person is not from God. Such a person has the spirit of the Antichrist, which you heard is coming into the world and indeed is already here.*

***But you belong to God, my dear children.** You have already won a victory over those people, because **the Spirit who lives in you is greater than the spirit who lives in the world.** Those people belong to this world, so they speak from the world's viewpoint, and the world listens to them. But we belong to God, and those who know God listen to us. If they do not belong to God, they do not listen to us. That is how we know if someone has the Spirit of truth or the spirit of deception.*
— 1 John 4:1-6 (New Living Translation)

*Dear friends, don't believe everyone who claims to have the Spirit of God. Test them all to find out if they really come from God. **Many false prophets have already gone out into the world,** and you can know which ones come from God. His Spirit says that Jesus Christ had a truly human body. But when someone doesn't say this about Jesus, you know that person has a Spirit that doesn't come from God and is the enemy of Christ. You knew that this enemy was coming into the world and now is already here.*

***Children, you belong to God,** and you have defeated these enemies. **God's Spirit is in you and is more powerful than the one that is in the world.** These enemies belong to this world, and the world listens to them, because they speak its language.*

We belong to God, and everyone who knows God will listen to us. That is how we can tell the Spirit that speaks the truth from the one who tells lies.
— 1 John 4:1-6 (Contemporary English Version)

* * * * * * * * *

"I'm scared. I think I just need to stay in here. Out there, I'll get in trouble. I just know I will. They all said I would, said I'm just made bad. Maybe they're right..." After five years in juvenile detention, Lora was to be released to a group home the next day. As she sat with Cassie, the facility's chaplain, she admitted her fears for the first time (ever).

Lora had learned well. Never let anyone know you're afraid. Ever. She'd also learned (she thought) that she was just born bad. Never mind the fact that her uncle gave her crack cocaine when she was nine. Never mind the fact she'd been the 'entertainment' at his parties. And never mind the fact that when she'd been **arrested for prostitution at age twelve**, no one had come to help her. No one. Not her uncle (who was wanted by the police himself), not her parents (who knew where they were anyway?), and definitely not her older sister, who had run away with a boyfriend years earlier.

As Cassie looked across the table at Lora, she saw a beautiful young woman with great possibilities and promise. If only....

"Lora, **can you remember anything good** from when you were little, you know, when you were three, four, maybe five years old?"

Lora sat and thought. She started to shake her head 'no', but then a small smile came to her face. **"Well, it's probably nothing, but..."** Cassie was intrigued - and glad to see her smile. "Let's hear it. You know, sometimes our 'nothings' are really worth a lot."

"OK. **Well, I remember when I was real little.** I remember being at my Grandma and Grandpa's house. They died, but..." Cassie quickly interrupted, trying to keep it positive. "But before that?"

Lora shook her head quickly, a forceful little back-and-forth motion. "Well, I must have been staying with them for the summer or something, 'cause **I remember baking cookies with Grandma.** She told everybody I was the best cookie maker she knew. She put this big tall chair up to the counter and let me stir and stuff. Know what else I just remembered?"

This was good. Cassie could remember baking with her Aunt May too, the smell of chocolate brownies filling the house....... "What, Lora?"

"She loved me. I know it. She told me so - said I was the best little girl ever."

"What about your Grandpa?" Knowing Lora's history, she almost hadn't dared ask the question, but something made her ask anyway. **"Did you do special things with your grandpa too?"** Cassie had to make herself breathe as she waited for Lora's response.

Lora's eyes got a faraway look, and then she laughed, almost giggled! Cassie realized then that **she'd never heard Lora laugh - not once.**

"Oh yeah, **Grandpa had this funny goat he called Trouble.** The name fit, too! I used to ride it. Grandpa said I must be a really special little girl, 'cause Trouble didn't even <u>like</u> most people. That goat would run out to give me goat-kisses every morning too. Then he'd turn around and wait for Grandpa to put me on his back. And Grandpa had this old retired farm horse named Beggar; he was always begging for something - carrots, apples, sugar cubes, whatever. Grandpa used to take me for rides on Beggar. You know, he really loved me, and he told me so too. He said I was one of God's special creations. **I think he's the only guy who ever loved me - for the real, whole me."** She stopped talking, deep in thought.

Cassie wasn't going to let this opportunity go. No way. **"So Lora, you've been in court a lot, right?"** Lora nodded. "OK then, **ever heard of original evidence?"** Lora looked up, thinking. "Well, is that like evidence that no one's messed with, maybe evidence that's been there from the beginning?"

Cassie smiled. "Exactly. You know what? **Your grandparents gave you the best original evidence** of who you really are, Lora. Not what some people tried to make you into, but what and who God created you to be. **You are one of God's special creations, Lora, and you are loved.** God has a future and great hope for you too. Let's work together to discover what that is, OK?"

If Lora could point to one moment that changed her life forever, that short conversation would be it. And change her life it did. She went on to become a children's advocate, shepherding children through the court system - being that voice in their wilderness reminding them that they too were special and loved - the original evidence said so!

* * * * * * * * *

There are, as Scripture says, "many false prophets in the world". They refute and try to hide the "original evidence" that we were created and are loved by God. They try to convince us that we don't belong to God, that He didn't send Jesus to show us how to live in the Spirit planted in each of us.

Sometimes we, like Lora, need to be reminded of this "original evidence". When we claim and live into the powerful presence of the Holy Spirit in our lives, we can discover and use the unique gifts and talents God created in us - living joyful lives of purpose and fulfillment.

Yes, we belong to God. The loving, grace-filled "original evidence" says so.
So let's fill our lives with that evidence of grace, love, and joy!

Reflections

What real-life "false prophets" can you think of? How do they affect people?

Why are many of us like Lora - we just don't claim God's "origin-al evidence" in our own lives?

What do you think Lora meant when she said of her Grandpa, "I think he's the only guy who ever loved me - for the real, whole me." ?

If you were Cassie, what would you tell Lora?

43

The Love Virus

Beloved, let us love one another, because love is from God; everyone who loves is born of God and knows God. Whoever does not love does not know God, for **God is love.** *God's love was revealed among us in this way: God sent his only Son into the world so that we might live through him. In this is love, not that we loved God but that he loved us and sent his Son to be the atoning sacrifice for our sins.*

Beloved, since God loved us so much, we also ought to love one another. No one has ever seen God; if we love one another, God lives in us, and his love is perfected in us.

- 1 John 4:7-12 (New Revised Standard Version)

Dear friends, let us continue to love one another, for love comes from God. Anyone who loves is a child of God and knows God. But anyone who does not love does not know God, for **God is love.** *God showed how much he loved us by sending his one and only Son into the world so that we might have eternal life through him. This is real love-not that we loved God, but that he loved us and sent his Son as a sacrifice to take away our sins.*

Dear friends, since God loved us that much, we surely ought to love each other. No one has ever seen God. But if we love each other, God lives in us, and his love is brought to full expression in us.

- 1 John 4:7-12 (New Living Translation)

* * * * * * * * * *

 As his second grade students left for the day, Ping turned to lesson planning. Science lesson planning. He loved science, always had, so he turned to the next unit with excitement. What would it be? As he turned the page, the subject seemed to jump out at him: **Viruses. *What?***

How was he supposed to teach seven and eight year olds about invisible things that multiply (still invisibly) and cause sickness and diseases (very visible) without them thinking it was all pretend, like the latest video game?

Only three months into his first year of teaching, Ping had an excellent mentor-colleague, so he went down the hall to Jolene's room. As he entered her classroom, he saw that she too was busy creating lesson plans. Seeing him, she put her pen down and looked up with a big smile. **"Hey Ping, how's it going?"**

"Viruses. I've got viruses." Lost in his own challenging thoughts, his words came out before he had a chance to really think them through. Jolene stayed behind her desk, instantly looking very worried. **"You've got viruses? More than one? Have you been to the doctor?"**

Ping laughed. "No, no. **I don't have them - they have me.** As in lesson planning about them!" Jolene laughed. "Glad we got <u>that</u> straight! Have a seat; let's talk it through. What's the most difficult thing to teach about them? Let's start there."

"That's easy," he began. "They're invisible - almost like magic (bad magic), and they make people sick. These kids, well, they're seven and eight. They surely won't get this."

Jolene thought a minute. As a fourth grade teacher, she had to think back a bit. Teaching about viruses to her students would be easier, she knew, but there had to be a way....maybe if... **"Hey Ping, how about asking the kids?** Ask them if they know of something that's invisible, spreads, and grows into something they can see. Then you can take it from there!"

"Hmmm. Risky, but then I like that kind of adventure. I'll try it. Thanks, Jolene. With that, Ping walked back to his classroom to finish the next week's plans.

Monday morning as science time began, Ping gathered his students in the science area at the back of the classroom. Taking a deep breath, he began. "OK kids, this science unit is going to be really cool. See if you can guess what it's going to be about. **First, does anyone know of something** that's invisible,...... spreads,..... and grows into something we can see?"

His class loved puzzled and riddles. They were great kids. Ping could tell they were thinking hard. "I know! I know!" Marta's small hand rose quickly and excitedly above her head, waving frantically at him to call on her. He nodded at her. **"I know, Mr. Ping. I learned about this yesterday.** It's really cool, too!"

"OK Marta. What do you think it is?"

"It's the Love Virus! My KidsPlace teacher told us all about it in church yesterday. It's like this: (Her face scrunched up in concentration.) Love is invisible, right?"

The class was all ears now, as **Marta ticked off the steps with her fingers.**
>*"One - love is invisible.*
>*Two - it spreads when we're together.*
>*Three - it makes us do really good, sometimes big things.*
>*Four - then we see it!*
So, it's the Love Virus!"

The virus lessons went very well after Marta's introduction. **In fact, it sparked a class project.** Ping's class adopted a kids' program at a local homeless shelter. They provided snacks, toys, and clothes for the children there. **The name of their project? The Love Virus, of course!**

✲ ✲ ✲ ✲ ✲ ✲ ✲ ✲ ✲

What would the world be like if Marta's "Love Virus" caught on and began to spread? That's the Kingdom question, and the Kingdom project! **We've got it -** the saving grace and love of Jesus. We are charged to love one another, to spread love wherever we go!

The world has many antidotes to this Love Virus. There are many ways, many choices we can make which will, in varying degrees and with varying success, keep the Love Virus away. But why would we want to keep from catching it?

I mean, **who wouldn't want to catch something** that would give them eternal, love-filled life at home with God? The answer is this: If people knew clearly and surely what this Love Virus really was, they'd all want to catch it. **The problem is that the world teaches that it's too good to be true. It's not.**

It's simple, and yet sometimes difficult, like Ping teaching that lesson. Listen again: *"Dear friends, since God loved us that much, we surely ought to love each other. No one has ever seen God. But if we love each other, God lives in us, and **his love is brought to full expression in us.**"*

Full expression. In us.

Let's try following Marta's advice:
> *"One - love is invisible."* True.
> *"Two - it spreads when we're together."* True, if we really behave with love, it will spread.
> *"Three - it makes us do really good, sometimes big things."* Oh yes, and those little things we do
>   for love really do add up pretty fast!
> *"Four - then we see it!"* Wouldn't that be great? We'd see God's rule breaking through and
>   growing stronger and bigger - right here and now!
> **"So, it's the Love Virus!"**

God IS love - catch it, and spread it!

Reflections

What would the world be like if Marta's "Love Virus" caught on and began to spread?

How can we help that happen?

Name some of the world's antidotes to the "Love Virus".

How does God answer each of the world's antidotes to the "Love Virus"?

44

Love-Standing

God has given us the Spirit. That is how we know that we are one with him, just as he is one with us. *God sent his Son to be the Savior of the world. We saw his Son and are now telling others about him. God stays one with everyone who openly says that Jesus is the Son of God. That's how we stay one with God and are sure that God loves us.*

God is love. If we keep on loving others, we will stay one in our hearts with God, and he will stay one with us. If we truly love others and live as Christ did in this world, we won't be worried about the day of judgment. A real love for others will chase those worries away. The thought of being punished is what makes us afraid. It shows that we have not really learned to love.

We love because God loved us first. But if we say that we love God and don't love each other, we are liars. We cannot see God. So how can we love God, if we don't love the people we can see? The commandment God has given us is: Love God and love each other!"   *- 1 John 4:13-21 (Contemporary English Version)*

This is how we know we're living steadily and deeply in him, and he in us: He's given us life from his life, from his very own Spirit. Also, we've seen for ourselves and continue to state openly that the Father sent his Son as Savior of the world. Everyone who confesses that Jesus is God's Son participates continuously in an intimate relationship with God. We know it so well, we've embraced it heart and soul, this love that comes from God.

God is love. When we take up permanent residence in a life of love, we live in God and God lives in us. This way, love has the run of the house, becomes at home and mature in us, so that we're free of worry on Judgment Day--our standing in the world is identical with Christ's. There is no room in love for fear. Well-formed love banishes fear. Since fear is crippling, a fearful life--fear of death, fear of judgment--is one not yet fully formed in love. We, though, are going to love--love and be loved. First we were loved, now we love. He loved us first. If anyone boasts, "I love God," and goes right on hating his brother or sister, thinking nothing of it, he is a liar. If he won't love the person he can see, how can he love the God he can't see? The command we have from Christ is blunt: Loving God includes loving people. You've got to love both.   *- 1 John 4: 13-21 (The Message Version)*

* * * * * * * * * *

"I love God. Really. It's people I can't stand!" This was the challenge laid down by one of the participants in the annual youth retreat. The speaker, Leon, had just read this Scripture and commented that it was not possible to love God without loving people. So Leon responded to the young man, intrigued by what might have caused him to respond so quickly. **"Tell us more. Is it all people you can't stand,** or just some people who maybe are unfair to you or give you a particularly hard time?"

Leon squinted his eyes to read the young man's name tag. "Mario. Sorry Mario, took me a minute to read your name tag - old man eyes and all." A bit of laughter defused some, but not all of the remaining tension the challenge had introduced into the room.

Mario seemed ready, and quite sure of his position. "Well, **God, I mean really....God is just always there.** People, come on now, they come and they go. You know, when the going gets tough, they just get going - know what I mean? You said you're old and all, so surely you get that!"

Leon thought about that for a minute. **"OK Mario, I'll give you that one.** <u>Sometimes</u> people don't stick around when hard times come. And yes, God always does - stick around, I mean."

Mario had a hard time not interrupting at the "sometimes" part, but he managed to wait until Leon took a breath. "<u>Sometimes</u> they don't stick around? Try pretty much <u>all</u> the time!"

Just then the kitchen crew called for lunch time, and Leon promised they'd continue the discussion later that evening when the group gathered for worship.

Mario got his food and approached the table where Leon was sitting. "Mind if I sit here?", he asked. Leon's answer surprised him. "Sure. Why not? Have a seat. Hey, and thanks for starting such a good discussion."

"You mean you're not mad or anything? Don't take this bad; I just couldn't help saying something. What you said - about loving people being proof that we love God - well, it just seems...sorry...but, <u>wrong</u>!"

Leon almost smiled, but then he saw how serious this young man was. **"So if what you're saying is that some people seem darned hard - OK maybe impossible - to love,** I agree. But loving them is not the same as liking them. It's not the same as liking what they do. And it's not the same as hanging out with them all the time either."

Yeah, I remember my Mom saying that kind of stuff all the time. But **God hangs out with us all the time, right?"** Leon nodded, prompting Mario to go on. Neither had taken more than a couple of bites of food.

"So maybe God doesn't like all the stuff we do - well, I know He doesn't - but **God stands by us anyway?"** Leon nodded again. Mario was on a roll now. **"So when we pray for people we don't really like too much, or...maybe for people who've hurt us...** That's like standing by them with God, right? That's a different kind of love. I think I'm starting to get this now!"

* * * * * * * * *

What Leon and Mario were talking about is our 'love-standing' before God. How willing are we to live into the love we know God has for us? How willing are we to be recognized as people who know God - as God's people. Have you ever heard the popular question, **"You got people?"** and the response, "I've got people!"? **If someone were to ask God,** "You got people?", would you be included in those He identified as His? How would another person recognize you as God's, as a Jesus-follower?

Loving people who love us is so much easier than loving those who are, well, let's say difficult to love. The writer of this First Letter of John knows that well. He knows what it's like to claim "permanent residence" in this life of God-love: *"When we take up permanent residence in a life of love, we live in God and God lives in us. This way, love has the run of the house, becomes at home and mature in us,* so that we're free of worry on Judgment Day--our standing in the world is identical with Christ's. There is no room in love for fear. Well-formed love banishes fear."*

The only way for God's love to "become at home and mature in us" is if we first let it in. We do have a choice. Will we open the door of our lives to that amazing love? Will we let it have "the run of the house"?

Remember: *"The command we have from Christ is blunt: Loving God includes loving people. You've got to love both."*

Reflections

If someone were to ask God, "You got people?", would you be included in those He identified as His? How would another person recognize you as God's, as a Jesus-follower?

Respond to this part of the Scripture: *"When we take up permanent residence in a life of love, we live in God and God lives in us. This way, love has the run of the house, becomes at home and mature in us,..."* Try putting it in your own words.

Respond to this pat of the Scripture: *There is no room in love for fear. Well-formed love banishes fear." Try putting it in your own words.*

45

Who Wins?

If we believe that Jesus is truly Christ, we are God's children. *Everyone who loves the father will also love the children. If we love and obey God, we know that we will love his children. We show our love for God by keeping his commandments, and they are not hard to follow.*

Every child of God can defeat the world, and our faith is what gives us this victory. *No one can defeat the world without having faith in Jesus as the Son of God.*

Water and blood came out from the side of Jesus Christ. It wasn't just water, but water and blood. The Spirit tells about this, because the Spirit is truthful. In fact, there are three who tell about it. They are the Spirit, the water, and the blood, and they all agree.

We believe what people tell us. But we can trust what God says even more, and God is the one who has spoken about his Son. If we have faith in God's Son, we have believed what God has said. But if we don't believe what God has said about his Son, it is the same as calling God a liar.

God has also said that he gave us eternal life and that this life comes to us from his Son. And so, ***if we have God's Son, we have this life.*** *But if we don't have the Son, we don't have this life.*

- 1 John 5:1-12 (*Contemporary English Version*)

* * * * * * * * * *

Good days. Bad days. That's what the doctor had told her. "You'll have good days when you'll remember everything you need to - and more. And then you'll have bad days when you might even forget how to do things you've been doing for years."

Alzheimer's. That's what they'd said. As Marissa sat at her kitchen table, she wished they'd said "cancer" instead. At least you got to keep your mind with cancer. **She'd always worried about getting cancer, but not...this.**

Marissa's husband Ray had died of cancer - lung cancer. *Why hadn't he stopped smoking?* But at least he'd known his own name when he died. Sometimes the ten years he'd been gone felt like a week; other times it seemed like forever.

She looked down at the table in front of her. **There they were - the pill bottles all lined up neatly in a row.** It really wouldn't take that long to swallow them. She had no children, and no brothers or sisters who lived close enough to check on her. Probably no one would even call for a few days. Oh, they'd miss her at the church women's luncheon, but that wasn't for another four days.

"The world can just win. I give up." Marissa hadn't even realized for a moment that she'd spoken the words out loud. Out loud into the silent, still kitchen air. Then it was as if the flood gates of her heart had burst. She laid it all out - out loud - before God that day at her kitchen table. Then she picked up the big cup of hot chocolate (her very favorite drink) and took a delicious sip. And then another.

Marissa picked up the first pill bottle. Valium. She'd just filled the prescription, so she knew there were thirty in there. She'd found another whole bottle just that morning as she gave the house a final cleaning. Her cousin had left it behind last summer. Marissa figured **there were fifty or so valium pills altogether. Yes, the world could win this one.** She'd just go to sleep - sweet sleep. No Alzheimer's for her - no sirree!

Then the phone rang. It was her sister Pam. **"You OK, sis? I got the strangest feeling just now.** It was like Ray was standing right behind me saying, 'Call Marissa. Now.' You know the way he was - a 'right now' kind of guy?" She assured Pam that, yes, she felt better than she had in years (and she did), said goodbye, and hung up.

Marissa opened the first pill bottle and dumped it into her favorite china dish. The pills looked beautiful against the pink roses of the dish. Just as she picked up the first two pills, **the phone rang again.** It was her nephew Ty in Seattle. "Hey, Aunt Riss," (He always called her that), "You OK? Weirdest thing. I was in my workshop building shelves - you know the ones Uncle Ray and I started way back? Well, I finally decided to finish them. So anyway, **there I was putting the brackets in when I thought I could hear him calling my name.** You know, like he used to do as soon as he got out of his car in the driveway? So I shook my head, thinking I'd better quit breathing those fumes in there or something. OK, so then I grabbed the saw to cut some wood, and man, **clear as day I heard him again. 'Call Aunt Riss', he said.** So, am I going crazy, Aunt Riss? You OK?"

"Sure Ty, I'm great. **You know your uncle, always a practical joker.** Now don't you worry about me. Finish those shelves - the cherrywood ones, right? Well I'm sure they'll be lovely. Bye now." And she hung up.

Am I going crazy? Marissa figured **she'd better swallow the pills fast** before something else strange happened. So she took another sip of the hot chocolate. Just as she reached into the pretty china dish for some of the pills, **the doorbell rang.** *What NOW?*

She quickly placed the dish and pill bottles in the cupboard. As she opened the door she saw - the mail carrier. What a dear young lady! She smiled at Marissa. **"Got a package here for you, Miss Marissa.** Mind if I stay a minute while you open it? **Return address is a bit odd,** that's all. I want to be sure it's OK - you mind?"

Taking the package, she invited the mail carrier, Lia, in. **Looking at the return address, Marissa felt her heart skip a beat.** It read:
Ray Blackstone
43 June Way
Midland, MI 48764

Ray? And from her own address? Lia saw her distress, took the package, and helped her sit at the kitchen table. **"Miss Marissa, can I get a cup of water?",** she asked. Her mind whirling as she stared at the package on the table in front of her, Marissa mumbled a "Sure...".

Lia opened the cupboard and held her breath as she saw the dish of pills and the bottles. Taking a glass, she closed the cupboard, filled it at the sink, and sat down with Marissa at the table.

"Lia, how can this be? Ray's been dead for years!"
"I know, ma'am, but this package, well, they're remodeling the downtown post office, and.... The zip code was a bit wrong, and it's been sitting there this whole time. It probably got stuck behind a shelf or something."

Marissa opened the package with shaking fingers. A present! She took it out of the mailing box and gently opened the beautiful daisy-flowered wrapping paper. Inside was a picture - a wonderful picture - of Ray. As she took in his smiling face, she read the words he'd written at the bottom:

"Faith wins, honey. Over everything. Don't ever give up, because God never gives up.
Love you, Baby. Ray."

* * * * * * * * *

"If we believe that Jesus is truly Christ, we are God's children.... Every child of God can defeat the world, and our faith is what gives us this victory."

Ray believed it. Marissa struggled. Pam, Ty, and Lia were God's hands and feet, voice and Spirit that day for her. God reached out in strong ways to claim her in one of her worst hours.

When we claim Christ, we inherit a host of spiritual sisters and brothers. Together we stand in Christ's name, in the Spirit's power, as saved children of God. We can defeat the world and its powers.

We need to remember that our time is not God's. **God's 'time' is forever, and through Christ that final victory has been won. Faith - and Jesus the Christ - rule!**

Reflections

What do you think of Ray's statement that, "Faith wins, honey. Over everything. Don't ever give up, because God never gives up."?

Who is winning in your life? How can you tell?

In what ways do you think we are called to be God's instruments of faith in the world?

46

Fax Faith?

I write these things to you who believe in the name of the Son of God, so that you may know that you have eternal life. And this is the boldness we have in him, that if we ask anything according to his will, he hears us. And if we know that he hears us in whatever we ask, we know that we have obtained the requests made of him.

If you see your brother or sister committing what is not a mortal sin, you will ask, and God will give life to such a one--to those whose sin is not mortal. There is sin that is mortal; I do not say that you should pray about that. All wrongdoing is sin, but there is sin that is not mortal. **We know that those who are born of God do not sin, but the one who was born of God protects them, and the evil one does not touch them.**

We know that we are God's children, and that the whole world lies under the power of the evil one. And we know that the Son of God has come and has given us understanding so that we may know him who is true; and we are in him who is true, in his Son Jesus Christ. **He is the true God and eternal life. Little children, keep yourselves from idols.**

- 1 John 5:13-21 (New Revised Standard Version)

I have written this to you who believe in the name of the Son of God, so that you may know you have eternal life. And we are confident that he hears us whenever we ask for anything that pleases him. And since we know he hears us when we make our requests, we also know that he will give us what we ask for.

If you see a Christian brother or sister sinning in a way that does not lead to death, you should pray, and God will give that person life. But there is a sin that leads to death, and I am not saying you should pray for those who commit it. All wicked actions are sin, but not every sin leads to death. **We know that God's children do not make a practice of sinning, for God's Son holds them securely, and the evil one cannot touch them.**

We know that we are children of God and that the world around us is under the control of the evil one. And we know that the Son of God has come, and he has given us understanding so that we can know the true God. And now we live in fellowship with the true God because we live in fellowship with his Son, Jesus Christ. **He is the only true God, and he is eternal life. Dear children, keep away from anything that might take God's place in your hearts.**

- 1 John 5:13-21 (New Living Translation)

* * * * * * * * *

152

"Oh, and we need to see your original birth certificate and your actual passport. We'll need three references - originals please - with signatures in colored (not black) ink. And by the way, our technicians can tell an original from a color copy. Any questions?"

A <u>lot</u> of questions came to Sali's mind, but none he'd dare ask. Questions like these: *Is it my foreign-sounding name? Do you do this to everyone? How do you ever fill these jobs?* **Do I really want this job?**

The last one was the real clincher for him. **Married with three children and the fourth due next month** - yes, he really did need the job! The pay was good, the hours were good, and it had full benefits, including health insurance, which they definitely needed.

"Can't I fax some of this to you? I mean, I live two hundred miles away...." The stern face of the human resources recruiter was answer enough, but just in case Sali didn't get it, she made it very plain.

"Look, Mr. ....Maitan, is it? Well, this is airport security you're applying for, OK? Originals, originals, originals. That's all we want; it's all we'll accept here. **No fakes, no faxes.** You do know what facsimile (fax) means, right?" She looked over the top of her glasses at him. "It means 'almost the original', a 'close copy of the original'. In other words - <u>almost</u> the original. **We don't specialize in 'almost'** around here. This is people's lives we're dealing with. The real deal."

She took a deep breath and continued. Sali settled in to listen, resigned to having to get all those original documents and trying to look polite and attentive though her lecture. After all, **he did need the job.**

"You don't want to be 'sort of' safe in the airport, right? How about if we 'almost' check the aircraft's safety? No? Didn't think so. Originals please."

Sali just stood and listened (really trying to keep his mouth from falling open and his eyes from glazing over). He realized that she was looking at him, expecting and answer, so he gave the expected, "Yes, ma'am," and waited for her to dismiss him.

"So, Mr. ...Maitan, any other questions? By the way, we've only got three openings. Better get your paperwork in quickly!"

Quickly. Right. Uh huh. "Yes, ma'am. Thanks for your help." As Sali left the office, he still felt a bit dazed. The two hundred mile trip home gave him time to think. **Did he want this job?** (He needed it.) Was it worth moving his family two hundred miles? (He needed the job.) OK, yes. Well.

So how would he gather all these papers in time? **He'd just have to get it done!** As he thought and planned, his mind ran back through the conversation he'd had with the recruiter. Sali had to admit to himself that he'd want the originals too - especially given the security risks these days.

As Sali drove on, he remembered something else. Something Pastor Joe had said last week. What <u>was</u> it? Oh yeah. **"Fax faith, almost real faith, isn't what God wants.** We need real, original faith - our unique and original 'yes' to Christ. Anything else means we're not worshipping God, we're really worshipping idols of our own choosing.'"

Security, he thought. **It really is about security.** *Thanks, God. Thanks for this lesson from a pretty unlikely source!*

* * * * * * * * *

So how would someone get caught in the "practice of sinning"? How could living in the ways of the "evil one" get to be so much of a habit that it becomes natural and not even noticed as unusual? Well, the more we accept "sort of", "close copies" or "almost" what God wants for us, the more we slide toward allowing other things to take the place of following Christ in our lives. **Before we know it, other things truly have taken God's place in our hearts.**

Sali's experience applying for a job in airport security called his attention to his eternal security. God used this situation in his life to help him examine where God was in his list of life's priorities. Some things are obviously not practices of a godly, Jesus-following life. Things like stealing, hurting others, and not spending time with God in prayer and Scripture. Others are more like "fax" issues. When we sort of treat others as neighbors the way Jesus teaches us, when we sort of pray (like when we're desperate about something), or when we know where our Bible is (perhaps on a bookshelf, maybe in a display place like on a table in our living room) but opening it would make the binding crack. These are more like "sort of", "almost", "facsimile" faith behaviors.

The problem with "fax faith" is that it becomes a habit. Soon we are moving God and a life of continuing discipleship to Christ down on our priority lists. Soon we really could be convicted of worshipping earthly idols. It's not a far step. **We need to stay in touch,** to keep our eternal, spiritual priority exactly, clearly, and authentically where it belongs: with God, as disciples (learners) of our Lord and Savior - Jesus the Christ!

Reflections

How would you describe "fax faith"? Give some real-world examples.

What are some ways we can keep from sliding into "fax faith"?

Second John

47

Due Diligence

*This letter is from John, the elder. I am writing to the chosen lady and to her children, whom I love in the truth-as does everyone else who knows the truth- because **the truth lives in us and will be with us forever.***

Grace, mercy, and peace, which come from God the Father and from Jesus Christ-the Son of the Father-will continue to be with us who live in truth and love. How happy I was to meet some of your children and find them living according to the truth, just as the Father commanded.

*I am writing to remind you, dear friends, that **we should love one another. This is not a new commandment, but one we have had from the beginning. Love means doing what God has commanded us,** and he has commanded us to love one another, just as you heard from the beginning.* - 2 John 1-6 (New Living Translation)

*My dear congregation, I, your pastor, love you in very truth. And I'm not alone--**everyone who knows the Truth that has taken up permanent residence in us loves you.***

*Let grace, mercy, and peace be with us in truth and love from God the Father and from Jesus Christ, Son of the Father! **I can't tell you how happy I am to learn that many members of your congregation are diligent in living out the Truth,** exactly as commanded by the Father.*

*But permit me a reminder, friends, and this is not a new commandment but simply a repetition of our **original and basic charter: that we love each other.** Love means following his commandments, and **his unifying commandment is that you conduct your lives in love.** This is the first thing you heard, and nothing has changed.* - 2 John 1-6 (The Message Version)

* * * * * * * * * *

"Hang him out to dry, that's what I say!" Jade passionately addressed the company's top leadership team. **"It's obvious he's the one.** I mean, Dennis is the guy who records the numbers, right?" They sat around the conference table, called to this emergency meeting when an **audit turned up thousands of dollars in missing revenue.**

All of them seemed to nod in agreement - except one: Dale. He sat with his hands folded in front of him, looking around the table at each team member. "I understand," he said. "We have reason to be worried. We have reason to be upset - angry even. But I have one question. Any of you ever been unjustly accused of anything? Further, any of you been fired and <u>then</u> found innocent?"

Blank looks were the only answers he received, so he continued. **"So I have two words for us: due diligence.** It means we stop. It means we look. We ask questions. We listen. And we investigate. Dennis doesn't handle the money. All he does is record the receipts management gives him. He never <u>sees</u> the money. All we have to do is <u>stop</u> and <u>think</u> to see that. Maybe he <u>does</u> know something. Maybe not. Making him the scapegoat won't help us find the answers we need. And guess what? **He may just turn around and sue us - ever think of that?"**

The expressions around the table told Dale the clear answer to that one: **no, they hadn't.**

Not to be deterred too long, Jade jumped right back into the conversation. "But I <u>know</u> both the managers there. They would <u>never</u> do something like this. **It has to be Dennis.** He got his hands on that money - somehow. Did you all know he's planning a vacation to Europe? Now just how does a convenience store clerk and bookkeeper afford that? **I'm telling you, he's guilty. End of story.** I say we call the cops now."

Dale was amazed - and more than irritated. "Let me check something out right now." He reached over to the conference room telephone on the table, pressed the speaker phone option, and dialed a number.

They all heard two rings and then the answer. **"Store 4782. Jan speaking. How may I help you today?"** *Good,* Dale thought, *Jan's the head cashier - she knows everyone and everything.* Dale asked her a simple question, "Hey Jan, Dale from the management team here. Is Dennis around? I heard he's going to Europe on vacation - wow! I didn't miss him, did I?"

Jan's response was very interesting - and enlightening. **"Didn't you hear about his uncle? The one who died** last month before he could take his dream vacation? Well, Dennis inherited that vacation! Cool, huh? Anyway, he'll be in later - 4PM, I think. You can call back then, OK?"

Dale smiled. "OK Jan. Thanks." As he hung up the phone, **Dale turned to the team. "Like I said, due diligence.** Sometimes we don't know what, or who, too well. We just <u>think</u> we do."

* * * * * * * * * *

"I can't tell you how happy I am to learn that many members of your congregation are diligent in living out the Truth,..." This Scripture writer is commending these followers because they live their faith "diligently". That is, they are conscious of their everyday choices. They measure their decisions based on their identity as followers of Christ. He reminds them that their "original and basic charter" is to conduct their lives in love.

If Jesus could 'tag along' with you, say, for just a day, what would He see? Would He say how happy He is to see you "living out the Truth" and conducting your life in love? Most of us (OK all of us) could point to **parts of yesterday that Jesus would be quite happy with.** We'd say, "Sure, Jesus could say that...about that part of my day...but..." Before we grind ourselves down over the parts of our day that wouldn't meet that criteria, let's remember this: **If we were perfect, we wouldn't need Jesus.**

Notice that this Scripture writer, **even after praising these folks, feels the need to remind them where their lives are to be grounded - in love.** They are to live in "due diligence" to their original rule. After all, God creates in love. God showers grace on us in love. **God sent Jesus out of love for us. Call it God's holy "due diligence".**

So how are we doing with our "due diligence"? Do we regularly "audit" (examine) our thoughts, words, and actions? Do we submit them to Christ, asking Him to teach us with His grace through those times we aren't so "diligent"?

If the "Truth has taken up permanent residence in us", let's let His truth and love indeed rule our lives as our "basic charter" that this Scripture speaks of!

Reflections

How would you describe "due diligence" with regard to our faith life? Our life as Christ-followers?

If "Truth takes up permanent residence in us", what does that look like?

"If we were perfect, we wouldn't need Jesus." What do you think of this statement?

How do you handle times in your life when you discover your faith's "due diligence" slipping?

48

Intruder Alert!

Many deceivers have gone out into the world, those who do not confess that Jesus Christ has come in the flesh; any such person is the deceiver and the antichrist! ***Be on your guard,*** so that you do not lose what we have worked for, but may receive a full reward. *Everyone who does not abide in the teaching of Christ, but goes beyond it, does not have God; whoever abides in the teaching has both the Father and the Son.*

Do not receive into the house or welcome anyone who comes to you and does not bring this teaching; for to welcome is to participate in the evil deeds of such a person. *Although I have much to write to you, I would rather not use paper and ink; instead I hope to come to you and talk with you face to face, so that our joy may be complete. The children of your elect sister send you their greetings.* — 2 John 7-13 (New Revised Standard Version)

Many liars have gone out into the world. *These deceitful liars are saying that Jesus Christ did not have a truly human body. But they are liars and enemies of Christ.* ***So be sure not to lose what we have worked for.*** *If you do, you won't be given your full reward. Don't keep changing what you were taught about Christ, or else God will no longer be with you. But if you hold firmly to what you were taught, both the Father and the Son will be with you.*

If people won't agree to this teaching, don't welcome them into your home or even greet them. *Greeting them is the same as taking part in their evil deeds. I have much more to tell you, but I don't want to write it with pen and ink. I want to come and tell you in person, because that will make us really happy. Greetings from the children of your very special sister.* — 2 John 7-13 (Contemporary English Version)

* * * * * * * * * *

It seemed so simple - and so fun. She'd just have a few friends over for a party. **Mom was gone for the weekend** - what she didn't know wouldn't hurt her, right?

What Jill hadn't counted on was the fact that the house was clearly visible from the apartment complex down the street. She hadn't thought through all the possibilities, such as:

   What if *some of the teens from those apartments notice the 'get together' at her house?*
   What if *they decide to come and check it out?*
   What if *they bring, say, alcohol and smokes (of varying kinds)?*
   What if *things get way out of hand?*

What if *the house ends up a big mess?*
What if *Mom comes home just a little sooner than expected?*

So Jill's plan began - and turned out far differently than she ever expected. Mom came home to some interesting discoveries:

- *glasses with alcoholic drinks still in them, stashed in cupboards, behind and under furniture.*
- *full ashtrays under furniture*
- *interesting rearrangements of furniture*
- *and more....*

 After arriving and making some of those interesting discoveries, Mom asked Jill: "What happened?"
"Oh my gosh, Mom, I never thought this would happen. Those kids just came over. Before I knew what was happening, they just...."

That day, Jill learned the importance of thinking ahead. She learned about planning, imagining possibilities, probabilities, and consequences. Jill also learned a very important life lesson: **There are "intruders" everywhere, not just at parties,** but in life in general. It's not always easy to "keep them out of your house", as Scripture warns us to do. Sometimes these "intruders" slip in, unnoticed until they make themselves known - usually in unpleasant ways.

While the instruction, *"Do not receive into the house or welcome anyone who comes to you and does not bring this teaching; for to welcome is to participate in the evil deeds of such a person."* **may seem particularly harsh, it is true.** Many times it seems that the closer we are walking in God's grace, love, and purpose for our lives, the more determined these "intruders" are to get in the middle and ruin things. **We must always be on the lookout.** We must always stay connected to God, because God will open our eyes and give us the wisdom and sight we need to recognize these "intruders" in time - for what they really are. **Once we recognize them,** we can rely on the presence and power of God's Holy Spirit to defeat them.

Better yet, as we grow and deepen our relationship with God through Jesus the Christ, we will become more and more able to recognize the "intruders" as they approach. **We'll be able to take "holy evasive action"!**

So spend time with God this week. Pray. Read Scripture. Share with Christian friends.

Be spiritually awake and aware for the next "intruder alert!" from God.

Reflections

What kind of "intruder alerts" does God give us?

How would you describe "holy evasive action"?

Reflections (continued)

Why would spending time with God in prayer and Scripture study, as well as with Christian friends, help us more easily identify these "intruders" in our lives?

Third John

49

Strange Hospitality

The elder to the beloved Gaius, whom I love in truth. Beloved, I pray that all may go well with you and that you may be in good health, just as it is well with your soul. **I was overjoyed when some of the friends arrived and testified to your faithfulness to the truth, namely how you walk in the truth.** *I have no greater joy than this, to hear that my children are walking in the truth.*

Beloved, **you do faithfully whatever you do for the friends, even though they are strangers to you;** *they have testified to your love before the church. You will do well to send them on in a manner worthy of God; for they began their journey for the sake of Christ, accepting no support from non-believers. Therefore we ought to support such people, so that we may become co-workers with the truth.*   *- 3 John 1-8 (New Revised Standard Version)*

The Pastor, to my good friend Gaius: How truly I love you! We're the best of friends, and I pray for good fortune in everything you do, and for your good health--that your everyday affairs prosper, as well as your soul! **I was most happy when some friends arrived and brought the news that you persist in following the way of Truth.** *Nothing could make me happier than getting reports that my children continue diligently in the way of Truth!*

Dear friend, **when you extend hospitality to Christian brothers and sisters, even when they are strangers, you make the faith visible.** *They've made a full report back to the church here, a message about your love. It's good work you're doing, helping these travelers on their way, hospitality worthy of God himself! They set out under the banner of the Name, and get no help from unbelievers. So they deserve any support we can give them. In providing meals and a bed, we become their companions in spreading the Truth.*

- 3 John 1-8 (The Message Version)

* * * * * * * * * *

It was an interesting sight. Just as Del and Carl finished getting the "Jesus on the Road Church" set up, they saw him walking down the ramp into the highway rest stop. **"Hey Del, would you look at that guy?** Wonder how far he's walked. From the look of him, must be a far piece of road he's covered!"

As Carl looked up, he saw the guy. **Wow. He did look pretty messed up.** Worn boots, sunburned face, and not walking too steady either. Carl finished pulling out the ramp leading up into the traveling 'church in a semi', as they called it. **Its official name was the Jesus on the Road Church,** because every Sunday it pulled into four rest stops and then the truck stop on the edge of town for worship. At two in the afternoon, this was the last rest stop worship for Pastors Del and Carl before they headed for the truck stop service at eight that evening, so they'd have some Sabbath rest time for themselves after this service.

Carl called out to Del at the other end of the 'church in a semi'. **"Hey, let's go help that guy.** Looks like he's getting slow. Stumbling a fair bit too. Come on!" So the two men headed down the ramp toward the man. As they got closer, **Carl yelled a friendly, "Howdy!", but got no answer.** Just as they reached the man, he almost collapsed in their arms. With Del on one side and Carl on the other, they helped him back to the church.

On the way to the church, they learned several things about this guy. First, he didn't speak English too well - in fact, he seemed to speak a language they'd never heard! Second, he motioned that his car was broken down on the highway and he'd walked five miles. **Five miles in hundred degree weather?** It was a miracle that he hadn't already passed out on the side of the road. Carl knew if it was him, his blond hair and freckles would have meant human toast around mile two. **But looking at this man's very dark skin, he marveled that he didn't bake at mile number one!**

Carl and Del helped the man into the cool air conditioning of the Jesus on the Road Church, and Del went to get him a drink of water. As he sipped, they took his boots off and Carl got a bucket of cool water. As his feet soaked, he began to recover. He pointed to himself and said, **"I am Buni. I am missionary from Sudan. I visit Second Baptist Church this night, six on the clock, to thank them for much support. Good people there. You know them?"**

Del answered. "Good to meet you brother. Can't say as we know them personally, but **they're brothers and sisters in Christ to us. All of us here to spread Jesus, right?"** Buni concentrated hard to understand what Del was saying.

Carl, whose sister had married a guy from Bosnia, understood how to "talk simple, with hands", as his new brother-in-law always said. He smiled at Buni (and got an instant smile in return). **In very simple words, and with lots of gestures, he said, "You worship with us. We take you to Second Baptist. We worship with you."** Buni understood that, a huge smile lighting up his face.

Buni kept his feet in that cool bucket all the way through worship at the rest stop. Carl brought the Lord's Supper to him in his seat and noticed the tears of joy in Buni's eyes as he received it. **When the truckers (and some summer tourists) learned about Buni, they did three things.** First, they gathered around him and prayed for him and God's work through him. Second, one of the tourists had an RV with just enough water for a shower and fresh clothes that fit Buni well. Third, all but a very few of them followed the Jesus on the Road Church to Second Baptist for evening worship.

Imagine the surprise in the eyes of that thirty (or so) member Baptist church as they saw <u>that</u> convoy coming up the road!

Buni was invited to give his testimony that evening, and this is what he said: "I am Buni, your missionary partner from Sudan. **These are my friends of strange hospitality of Jesus.** They say you brothers and sisters in Christ for them. They have Jesus on the Road Church." He looked over at Del to be sure he had the name right. When Del nodded, he continued.

"Please excuse English. Strange hospitality people speak Jesus-talk. Everybody understand that language. I hope when I go you can all give more strange hospitality - like Jesus on the Road Church. God bless you much." As Buni sat down, Del realized that Buni hadn't asked for more support for himself. He'd been doing his best to testify about <u>their</u> church!

Buni came to say thank you and obtain continued support for his mission work in Sudan. What he got was so much more. **The "strange hospitality" he spoke of that night developed into a wonderful partnership** between Buni's Sudan church, the Second Baptist Church, and the Jesus on the Road Church. All that from a bucket of cool water and an invitation.

✱ ✱ ✱ ✱ ✱ ✱ ✱ ✱ ✱

"Dear friend, **when you extend hospitality to Christian brothers and sisters, even when they are strangers, you make the faith visible.** *They've made a full report back to the church here, a message about your love. It's good work you're doing, helping these travelers on their way,* **hospitality worthy of God himself!"**

What seemed like a one time, helping a brother kind of ministry turned into a whole lot more for these new ministry partners. **Who would have thought?** (God.) Who would have ever imagined that these very different, pretty unlikely partners in ministry would meet and develop such a powerful and effective means of spreading the Good News of Christ? (God.)

What amazing, holy transformation would bless our lives and the world around us if we all just learned and practiced more "strange hospitality" and "Jesus-talk"!

Reflections

Why do you think Buni described the way he was treated as "strange hospitality"?

What sort of language is the "Jesus-talk" Buni refers to?

Have you ever extended "strange hospitality" or had it extended to you? What was that like?

If you are involved in a church, does it practice "strange hospitality" and/or "Jesus-talk"? If so, how? If not, why do you think that is?

50

Model-Building

I wrote to the church. But Diotrephes likes to be the number-one leader, and he won't pay any attention to us. So if I come, I will remind him of how he has been attacking us with gossip. Not only has he been doing this, but he refuses to welcome any of the Lord's followers who come by. And when other church members want to welcome them, he puts them out of the church.

__Dear friend, don't copy the evil deeds of others! Follow the example of people who do kind deeds.__ They are God's children, but those who are always doing evil have never seen God.

Everyone speaks well of Demetrius, and so does the true message that he teaches. I also speak well of him, and you know what I say is true.

I have so much more to say to you, but I don't want to write it with pen and ink. I hope to see you soon, and then we can talk in person. I pray that God will bless you with peace! Your friends send their greetings. Please give a personal greeting to each of our friends.

- 3 John 9-15 (Contemporary English Version)

Earlier I wrote something along this line to the church, but Diotrephes, who loves being in charge, denigrates my counsel. If I come, you can be sure I'll hold him to account for spreading vicious rumors about us. As if that weren't bad enough, he not only refuses hospitality to traveling Christians but tries to stop others from welcoming them. Worse yet, instead of inviting them in he throws them out.

__Friend, don't go along with evil. Model the good. The person who does good does God's work.__ The person who does evil falsifies God, doesn't know the first thing about God. Everyone has a good word for Demetrius--the Truth itself stands up for Demetrius! We concur, and you know we don't hand out endorsements lightly. I have a lot more things to tell you, but I'd rather not use pen and ink. I hope to be there soon in person and have a heart-to-heart talk.

- 3 John 9-15 (The Message Version)

* * * * * * * * * *

"But Dad! The Pinewood **Derby's next week, and Frank says his car's gonna beat mine** - and everybody else's - by <u>miles</u>! It's just not fair! I know his dad built his, 'cause he was bragging about it all over school!" Kurt put his hands on his hips, doing his best imitation of "Bratty Frank", as he often called this kid. **"My dad's better than your dad,"** he chanted (for effect) as he looked at his dad. "<u>My</u> dad's better than <u>your</u> dad.

Just wait till you see <u>our</u> car. Bet <u>your</u> dad won't build a car for <u>you</u>. You're gonna lose too - big time! **Loser! Loser!"** Kurt dropped his hands to his sides, a pleading look on his face. "That's how it is every <u>day</u>, Dad. Bratty Frank's <u>got</u> to lose! Come on, dad! I <u>know</u> **Frank's not the only one whose dad's helping him build his car.** How can I win? Please? Pleeeeeeease?"

Terry motioned Kurt into the dining room. "Have a seat, son." They both sat down. Terry understood, really, but.... **"So, son, whose race is this?** I'd love to build a car for the Parent's Race, but which race do <u>you</u> want to enter?"

"But Dad!!"

"No 'but dads' about it, son. **If I did build <u>your</u> car, what would I be teaching you?** You're growing up fine, great in fact. You're honest, hard-working, and (most times) fun to be with. Why would I want to ruin that?"

Kurt sighed (OK, blew out air would be a better description). "I wouldn't get <u>ruined</u>, Dad. I promise!" Kurt raised his hand in the Cub Scout salute.

Terry smiled. "Exactly. Hold that pose for me for a second. Doesn't the Cub Scout Promise say something about honesty? Mmmm hmmm. Thought so. **How honest would it be for me to do what you're asking?"**

Kurt slowly lowered his hand, his face solemn. "Not very honest, I guess. OK, Dad. As he started to get up, Kurt thought of something. "I know! Let's <u>both</u> build cars! I bet your car can beat any of the other dads' cars - you build <u>great</u> stuff, Dad!"

A week later, Kurt and his Dad entered their cars in the Cub Scout Pinewood Derby races. Neither won first place (Kurt took second; Terry third), but they had a great time building and racing their cars together.

The "modeling" that happened that week would last a lifetime. In fact, this story was told by Kurt to <u>his</u> son a generation later.

* * * * * * * * *

Terry. Kurt. Kurt's son. Kurt's son's son..... **Who knows how far** this example of modeling God's way will travel? Who knows how many will eventually experience and learn from Terry's modeling in the kitchen and in that Cub Scout event?

Godly, Christ-following model-building goes a long way. As this Scripture instructs us, *"**Model the good. The person who does good does God's work.** The person who does evil falsifies God, doesn't know the first thing about God."*

Godly, Christ-following model-building, modeling, and model-following goes a long way.
Thousands of years; eternity in fact. Think about it.
How much holy, Christ-like modeling are you involved in?

Reflections

Think of someone you know who "models the good". Describe the effects their modeling has on those around them.

What would Christ-like modeling look like? What effect would it have?

How much holy, Christ-like modeling are you involved in? How could you be involved in more?

51

Behind Holy Lines

Jude, a servant of Jesus Christ and brother of James, To those who are called, who are beloved in God the Father and kept safe for Jesus Christ: May mercy, peace, and love be yours in abundance.

Beloved, while eagerly preparing to write to you about the salvation we share, I find it necessary to write and appeal to you to contend for the faith that was once for all entrusted to the saints. **For certain intruders have stolen in among you,** *people who long ago were designated for this condemnation as ungodly,* **who pervert the grace of our God into licentiousness and deny our only Master and Lord, Jesus Christ.**

Now I desire to remind you, though you are fully informed, that the Lord, who once for all saved a people out of the land of Egypt, afterward destroyed those who did not believe. And the angels who did not keep their own position, but left their proper dwelling, he has kept in eternal chains in deepest darkness for the judgment of the great day. Likewise, Sodom and Gomorrah and the surrounding cities, which, in the same manner as they, indulged in sexual immorality and pursued unnatural lust, serve as an example by undergoing a punishment of eternal fire.

- Jude 1-7 (New Revised Standard Version)

From Jude, a servant of Jesus Christ and the brother of James, to all who are chosen and loved by God the father and are kept safe by Jesus Christ. I pray that God will greatly bless you with kindness, peace, and love!

My dear friends, I really wanted to write you about God's saving power at work in our lives. But instead, I must write and ask you to defend the faith that God has once for all given to his people.

Some godless people have sneaked in among us and are saying, "God treats us so much better than we deserve, and so it is all right to be immoral." They even deny that we must obey Jesus Christ as our only Master and Lord. But long ago the Scriptures warned that these godless people were doomed.

Don't forget what happened to those people that the Lord rescued from Egypt. Some of them did not have faith, and he later destroyed them. You also know about the angels who didn't do their work and left their proper places. God chained them with everlasting chains and is now keeping them in dark pits until the great day of judgment. We should also be warned by what happened to the cities of Sodom and Gomorrah and the nearby towns. Their people became immoral and did all sorts of sexual sins. Then God made an example of them and punished them with eternal fire.

- Jude 1-7 (Contemporary English Version)

* * * * * * * * * *

"Church? You're getting involved in church? Oh man, you'd better watch out. Don't get too caught up in that. Some of those people - they're really messed up. I've been to some of those places, and there's **no way I'm making that mistake again!"**

Wow! Brice hadn't expected his neighbor's strong response. **Zane had invited him on a guys' fishing trip the next weekend - the same weekend of the annual church carnival.** Brice had recently started getting active in a local church after years of staying away. So far it had been good, and when one of the leaders asked if he'd be willing to coordinate and run the hot dog wagon, he'd said yes. **What should he say to Zane?** He knew exactly what Zane was talking about - been there, done that. He even had a couple of old (really old) t-shirts in his workshop rag box to prove it. They'd be...let's see...about twenty years old by now.

"Well, Zane, thanks again for the invite. You know, I've met - even worked with - some pretty 'messed up' people', as you said. That wasn't in any church, either!" He smiled, and Zane chuckled, nodding agreement. "Me too, neighbor, me too. But **I just expected different things in a church.** I mean, the things they said - and did - even in the church building! Those things weren't even close to what Jesus taught. No way, no how! **Hey, you've heard of being 'behind enemy lines', right? Well, something got in 'behind their holy lines'!"**

Now it was Brice's turn to chuckle. **"Ah, so you had 'intruders' in your old church huh? Me too, me too. They're everywhere.** I really like your 'behind holy lines' thing too. You're right. In fact, we were just reading about that in the men's Bible study yesterday, about how even in the very first churches, people had to be warned to look out for those kind of intruders. That's why it's so important to stay informed and alert, so you don't get sucked in - or driven out - by them. Because, you know what? They definitely do not have Christ's way in them. If they did, then they sure wouldn't act that way." It looked like Zane was interested, so he continued.

"Oh, and one more thing, not to be preachy or anything, but....you know we're all 'messed up' in some way, right? I think if we were all perfect, then we wouldn't need church for sure, and not Jesus either, for that matter. Anyway, **I hope you're going fishing another weekend too, because I'd love to come along."**

To be honest, Zane's eyes had sort of glazed over about half-way through this part of Brice's little 'speech', but **pieces of what Brice had said kept coming to him all weekend** as he and some of the neighborhood men fished and relaxed. When one of the guys asked about Brice, Zane explained that maybe he'd get to join them next time - probably next month. **Then Zane asked something he never, ever could have imagined asking anyone a week before.** As they sat around the fire frying fish, he asked, "Hey, anybody go to church?" Zane discovered something he'd never known before. The guy two doors down the street from him was a retired missionary! Zane shared what Brice had told him (what he could remember anyway) and was surprised at the great discussion that followed. **The guys especially liked his 'behind holy lines' description.**

The next month more men (some from Brice's church) joined the "fishing group", and they came up with a name for themselves: **"Men Chasing Fish Chasing Men".** The name came out of the continuing discussion about where 'enemy lines' and 'holy lines' were, and what that meant.

Soon the guys decided to start a young men's fishing group. They helped and supported one another; many got to know Jesus for the first time, and many others renewed relationships with Him and got connected in local churches. They learned that people could act pretty human, and yes, pretty "messed up" at times, but **knowing where the 'holy lines' were was vital. This painted a new picture of possibility for church as far as Zane was concerned.**

* * * * * * * * * *

Where are the 'enemy lines' and 'holy lines' in your life? We all have them. Where do you feel temptations to act in ways that would "deny our only Master and Lord, Jesus Christ"?
Those are your 'enemy lines'!

Where do you experience Christ reaching people through you? Where are you at your best as God's instrument of transforming grace? Those are your 'holy lines'.

This is the assignment Jude is giving: once we've identified those 'lines', we are to hold the 'holy lines' strong and firm. Amazingly, the 'enemy lines' will become clearer as we do this, and we will feel incredible power as those enemy lines are weakened – and defeated!.

We'll experience God's awesome power - even 'behind enemy lines'!

Reflections

Where are the 'enemy lines' in your life? We all have them. Where do you feel temptations to act in ways that would "deny our only Master and Lord, Jesus Christ"?
Those are your "enemy lines"!

Where do you experience Christ reaching people through you? Where are you at your best as God's instrument of transforming grace? Those are your "holy lines".

What are some ways you can weaken the "enemy lines" and strengthen the "holy lines" in your life?

52

Lost in Time and Space

In the same way, these people-who claim authority from their dreams-live immoral lives, defy authority, and scoff at supernatural beings. But even Michael, one of the mightiest of the angels, did not dare accuse the devil of blasphemy, but simply said, "The Lord rebuke you!" (This took place when Michael was arguing with the devil about Moses' body.)

*But **these people scoff at things they do not understand. Like unthinking animals, they do whatever their instincts tell them, and so they bring about their own destruction.** What sorrow awaits them! For they follow in the footsteps of Cain, who killed his brother. Like Balaam, they deceive people for money. And like Korah, they perish in their rebellion.*

*When these people eat with you in your fellowship meals commemorating the Lord's love, **they are like dangerous reefs that can shipwreck you.***

***They are like shameless shepherds who care only for themselves.** They are like **clouds blowing over the land without giving any rain.** They are like **trees in autumn that are doubly dead,** for they bear no fruit and have been pulled up by the roots. They are like **wild waves of the sea,** churning up the foam of their shameful deeds.*

*They are like **wandering stars, doomed forever to blackest darkness.** Enoch, who lived in the seventh generation after Adam, prophesied about these people. He said, "Listen! The Lord is coming with countless thousands of his holy ones to execute judgment on the people of the world. He will convict every person of all the ungodly things they have done and for all the insults that ungodly sinners have spoken against him."*

***These people are grumblers and complainers, living only to satisfy their desires.** They brag loudly about themselves, and they flatter others to get what they want.*   *- Jude 8-16 (New Living Translation)*

*But **these people sneer at anything they can't understand, and by doing whatever they feel like doing-- living by animal instinct only--they participate in their own destruction.** I'm fed up with them! They've gone down Cain's road; they've been sucked into Balaam's error by greed; they're canceled out in Korah's rebellion.*

*These people are **warts on your love feasts** as you worship and eat together. They're giving you a black eye-- carousing shamelessly, grabbing anything that isn't nailed down.*

*They're--**puffs of smoke pushed by gusts of wind; late autumn trees stripped clean of leaf and fruit,** Doubly dead, pulled up by the roots; **wild ocean waves leaving nothing** on the beach but the foam of their shame; **lost stars in outer space on their way to the black hole.***   *- Jude 10-13 (The Message Version)*

* * * * * * * * * *

"So, what are we doing Sunday morning?" Meghan was in town visiting her sister for spring break. She was thinking that **Terri seemed somehow...different.**

Terri scrunched her face up - not a pleasant look to be sure. **"Oh yeah, I bet you want to go to church, right? Now there's money wasted."** She laughed - a hard brittle sound - way unfamiliar to Meghan, coming from her sister anyway.

As Meghan opened her mouth to speak, Terri spoke again. **"Speaking of wasted, I was hoping you'd go with me to a great party tomorrow night.** It _is_ Saturday, you know. You do remember Saturday nights, right? We're celebrating the twins' twenty-first birthday!"

Meghan thought back to their last phone conversation. *Twins....twins...**oh yes, the 'Party Band Twins**" Terri kept going on (and on) about....oh boy.*

"Yeah sis, now there's getting something for your money! We're going down to Band Club Row, gonna see how many bands we can hear. Know what mean? Sis? Hey _Sis_? Hello? You in there?"

"Sure, Terri, sure. What I don't get is...well, **how is that not wasting money?** I mean, you don't even remember most of it by morning, right? And how is getting drunk going to really help anyone?"

Uh oh. Meghan could see from Terri's face this was <u>not</u> going to be good.

"Whatever. You just stay at my place and paint your nails for church or what<u>ever</u>. But you'll miss out - big time! Oh, and **then you can waste your money tomorrow at that church of yours.** Hey, that's it. Exactly <u>what</u> do you have to show for <u>that</u> money? Uh huh. Thought so. All I ever got out of church was zip, nada, nothing. Good luck with <u>that</u> one, Sis!"

So Terri went partying and Meghan stayed home checking out local churches on the internet, reading her Bible, and hanging out in her favorite online Christian singles chat room.

Meghan woke up several times that night, each time looking at the alarm clock by the bed. Midnight. 2AM. 3AM. No Terri. Her mind bounced back and forth between imagining Terri in a ditch somewhere and the picture of her passed out at some friend's (or more likely acquaintance's) place.

4AM. 6AM. No answer on Terri's cell phone. Then the apartment phone rang - a harsh noise in the silent, anxiety-ridden atmosphere. She waited for the machine to answer (not her phone...), then to see if whoever was calling would leave a message. They did.

"Hello? **This is the Central Hospital Emergency Department** calling for any relatives of Teresa....Johnson...?" Meghan snatched the phone and answered it. *Oh God,....* "This is her sister, Meghan. Is she OK?" The young man on the other end of the line paused, and Meghan's anxiety level shot up higher as he asked the next question. **"Well, ma'am...would you please spell your name for me?"**

What now? Was this one of Terri's practical jokes? Where was Terri, anyway? "OK. Here it is: M-e-g-h-a-n J-o-h-n-s-o-n. Is my sister OK? Could you please tell me?"

"Well, Ms. Johnson...may I call you Meghan...?"

Meghan pinched herself to be sure she was really awake. *Oh God, let this be a dream, please.* "Sure you can, but... **Is my sister OK?"**

"Meghan, **they found her car this morning.** Seems she lost control out on I-70. Near as they can figure, she went over the edge and rolled down the side of the mountain out there. Someone in the car had enough strength left to dial 9-1-1 and we tracked them down. Meghan, do you know any of the people who were with your sister last night? We've identified one of them, but we've got two young men with no ID on them...can you help?"

Meghan almost stopped breathing. **"Identified? Can't Terri tell you?** I mean, if...."

"I'm so sorry, Meghan, but none of them made it. That car rolled at least seven times, maybe eight before it landed. That's why **it took so long to find it at the bottom of the cliff."**

Bottom of the cliff? Seven or eight times? None of them made it? Oh God. **What a waste, indeed.**

The drive to the hospital felt like the longest - and the shortest - drive she'd ever made. Time and space seemed to stand still, and **she felt literally sucked into a black hole, lost in a very, very bad dream.** Problem was, this was no dream.

Later as she talked with the hospital chaplain, she described her frustration with the direction Terri's life had gone in the last year. **"What could I have done?"**, she asked, tears streaming down her face. "She just wanted to have fun. **If it felt good, she did it.** And her eyes, they used to be so alive! When I got here, I almost didn't recognize her. **Her eyes, they looked...empty."** The chaplain sat with her as sobs shook her whole body. When she calmed a bit, Meghan shared how she'd felt during the long (but short) drive to the hospital. **"Lost in time and space, that's how it was. Never thought I'd feel lost, not as a Christian anyway. Isn't that all about being found?"**

"Well, Meghan. **There's lost, and then there's lost.** All of us <u>feel</u> lost sometimes, but lost doesn't necessarily mean alone. If you claim Christ, you are never alone, and you're never actually lost - not from what's really important in life."

"But what about Terri?" Meghan finally put into words her deepest fear for her sister. The chaplain thought a minute. "Well, that's between her and God. Only God and Terri know where her deepest self truly was. That's not for us to determine. We're just called to love her and love God. From the time we've spent together tonight, I'd say you're not lost at all. You loved, and you love, Terri very much. And you love God too."

* * * * * * * * * *

It's true. **We all have that 'lost in time and space' feeling sometimes.** There's a big difference between being lost <u>from</u> Christ and feeling lost <u>with</u> Christ. When He is our anchor, the center of our spiritual being, we are never truly alone.

This Scripture describes those who are so totally out of touch with Jesus that they can truthfully be described as *"clouds blowing over the land without giving any rain"*, *"trees in autumn that are doubly dead"*, *"wild waves of the sea, churning up the foam of their shameful deeds"*, and *"wandering stars, doomed forever to blackest darkness"*. **With no center, these people use their physical human instinct and temptations as a basis for decisions, words, and actions. They become more and more "lost in time and space".** Terri indeed *"participated in her own* *destruction"*, as this Scripture says.

Meghan walked with her sister anyway. She didn't make the same decisions Terri did, but she never stopped praying for her sister and never stopped showing her a Christ-centered life.

Who do we know that's like Terri? How can we pray for them and show them examples of a Christ-centered and joyful life?

Perhaps you know someone (maybe it's you) **who is, or has been, in Meghan's place.** How have you, or can you, show Christ's love and strength to them? I promise you that **as we put Christ's love and saving grace into action, less and less of our sisters and brothers will be....lost in time and space.**

Reflections

Who do we know that's like Terri? How can we pray for them and show them examples of a Christ-centered and joyful life?

How do we handle those times when we feel "lost in time and space"?

What resources does God give us in Christ to aid and strengthen us in those times?

53

Centered Life

But you, beloved, must remember the predictions of the apostles of our Lord Jesus Christ; for they said to you, "In the last time there will be scoffers, indulging their own ungodly lusts." It is these worldly people, devoid of the Spirit, who are causing divisions.

But you, beloved, build yourselves up on your most holy faith; pray in the Holy Spirit; keep yourselves in the love of God; look forward to the mercy of our Lord Jesus Christ that leads to eternal life. And have mercy on some who are wavering; save others by snatching them out of the fire; and have mercy on still others with fear, hating even the tunic defiled by their bodies.

Now to him who is able to keep you from falling, and to make you stand without blemish in the presence of his glory with rejoicing, to the only God our Savior, through Jesus Christ our Lord, be glory, majesty, power, and authority, before all time and now and forever. Amen. - Jude 17-25 (New Revised Standard Version)

But remember, dear friends, that the apostles of our Master, Jesus Christ, told us this would happen: "In the last days there will be people who don't take these things seriously anymore. They'll treat them like a joke, and make a religion of their own whims and lusts." These are the ones who split churches, thinking only of themselves. There's nothing to them, no sign of the Spirit!

But you, dear friends, carefully build yourselves up in this most holy faith by praying in the Holy Spirit, staying right at the center of God's love, keeping your arms open and outstretched, ready for the mercy of our Master, Jesus Christ. This is the unending life, the real life! Go easy on those who hesitate in the faith. Go after those who take the wrong way. Be tender with sinners, but not soft on sin. The sin itself stinks to high heaven.

And now to him who can keep you on your feet, standing tall in his bright presence, fresh and celebrating-- to our one God, our only Savior, through Jesus Christ, our Master, be glory, majesty, strength, and rule before all time, and now, and to the end of all time. Yes. - Jude 17-25 (The Message Version)

* * * * * * * * *

They'd been running around the campground all day, earning points in the annual youth rally competition. After all, big points meant big prizes! The youth had each received a list at the start of the weekend listing all the ways to earn points.

Drew had 'the look' - the one that said he had a lot of points (and he knew it). **The grand prize was** (drum roll...) **a one year, unlimited use pass to the fun center** (think arcade, bumper cars, and mini golf all in one place), and Drew was determined to win it.

"So Drew, how many latrines did you scrub today, anyway?" Rebecca winked at him as she asked. She'd seen him, cleaning supplies in hand, heading from the middle schoolers' latrines (gross!) down the hill toward the dining hall that morning. Drew rolled his eyes at her, smiling (she <u>was</u> cute!). "Oh, I figure at a hundred points a piece, let's see......" He consulted his score sheet. "Hmmm...fifteen latrines at a hundred each, that comes to....fifteen hundred points!"

Just then Corey and Mia, the youth leaders, came in with three green boxes. Jigsaw puzzles? The looks aimed their way were very confused. Several of the youth got their score sheets out, looking for <u>this</u>. Nope. No "jigsaw puzzle" listed...

Rebecca's expression was way different from the others. She got excited. "Whoo-hoo! I <u>love</u> puzzles. This must be the 'mystery event' at the bottom of our score sheets, right? **I'm all over this one - bring it on!"**

Corey smiled as he motioned for the youth to gather around the big round table in the center of the lodge's living room. "OK. Here's the deal. **We've got three of these puzzles. They're all the same....green! Oh, and they have bugs too!"**

As he paused, **Corey noticed a lot of "We knew he was weird; here's proof." looks,** but he continued explaining anyway. "So, each of your names is on a slip of paper in this hat. We'll pull them out into three piles, creating our teams. One team stays here, one goes to the dining hall, and the other to the rec hall. They all gathered around closer (probably looking for those bugs), leaning over the table to get a better view as names were drawn and placed in the three teams.

Brett (ever the detail kind of guy) **was the first to figure out that this wasn't as easy a task** as it might first seem. "Whoa there! Hey Mia, those puzzles really are all....green! Well, like Corey here said, green except for the......little bugs that are hiding in all that green grass! **This'll take more time than we have in the whole weekend!"** He looked at the edge of one of the puzzle boxes. "Great. A <u>thousand</u> pieces of this stuff too. Let me see something." **He pulled his scorecard out.** "A thousand points for the first team done?"

It was Mia's turn to smile now. "Well," she winked at them. **"There is a secret to putting these together.** That's all I'm going to say. The team that figures it out ought to be able to finish in..." She looked at her watch. 'Well, let's say in plenty of time for dinner an hour and a half from now!'

Each team took one of the puzzles and went to their assigned work areas. **Sure enough, just an hour later** Brett looked out the window of the dining hall and spotted the rec hall team out on the lawn playing frisbee! *What? How?*

The other two teams barely had the outer edges of their puzzles assembled when the dinner bell sounded. Drew was <u>not</u> happy. "Scratch our 1000 points for first place, and our 750 for second for sure." A <u>really</u> competitive guy, he wasn't even in the mood for the barbequed chicken dinner now.

As they settled in the dining hall to eat, Corey turned the sound system on and went to the microphone. "Well, we have a clear first place winner. **Rebecca's Puzzlers got the whole thing together in record time!** We counted put-together pieces in order to award second and third places. Second place, and 750 points, goes to.....

Jared's Jigsaw Bunch! Third place, and 500 points, goes to....Brett's Wish We Were Fishing team! **Now, would someone from the Puzzlers explain the secret?"**

Bonnie stood up, a twinkle in her eye. She walked over to the Jigsaw Bunch's puzzle table and picked up a couple of puzzle pieces, holding the backs up to the light. "Remember the Scripture themes for this weekend rally? Remember Psalm 139 and the book of Philemon? Well, **these are custom-made puzzles. If you start in the middle, the center that is, the center makes a cross - see the back sides?** Going out from there, around and around in bigger and bigger circles, are the words of our two weekend rally Scriptures. **So, put Jesus and His cross in the center, surround it with Scripture, and....you win!!"**

* * * * * * * * *

As we come to the close of this journey together through the "Little-Known New Testament", it is my hope and prayer that this part of the Bible isn't "little-known" to you any more.

As Bonnie found out, the Christian life is really about keeping Jesus in the center and the Scripture (with the Holy Spirit's teaching through it) around it, creating a life grounded in our discipleship to Christ and our ever-deepening, ever-closer relationship with God, powered and led by the Holy Spirit.

Think about your own life. How is Christ in the middle - or not? What does that mean to you?

What has this Scripture exploration meant for you? Has it changed your everyday experience of God? If so, how? If not, why do you think that is?

Above all, keep exploring with Christ. Keep experiencing His power in your life. Every day!

Reflections

How can we tell where a person's life is "centered"?

How close to the center of your life is Christ? How do you know?

Is the "little-known New Testament" any better known to you now than at the beginning of our study? If so, how? If not, why do you think this is?

Appendix 1

Bible Translations and How to Find Them

Four versions/translations of Scripture are used in the Exploring... Bible study series. One or more of them may have appealed to you as you read and experienced this book. You may wonder what's different about them. You may have decided you'd like to purchase one or more.

The information contained here should assist you in doing just that. Here is a brief description of each version/translation along with sources, should you decide to purchase one or more of them.

Contemporary English Version, published by the American Bible Society (ABS) in 1995, is available through them (www.bibles.com). Originally intended as a children's translation, it uses very simple, contemporary language which can be read and easily understood by those of all ages. The CEV is one of the versions recommended especially for those for whom English is a second language. The New Testament was translated directly from the Greek text; Psalms and Proverbs from the Masoretic Hebrew text; and the balance from their original languages as well.

New Revised Standard Version, published in 1989 by the National Council of Churches, is an updated version of the Revised Standard Version. The NRSV is available in most Christian and large volume bookstores, as well as from the American Bible Society (www.bibles.com). It is the most widely used ecumenical (used by many Christian traditions) version and is used in many seminaries. A committee of about thirty members of various Protestant denominations and the Roman Catholic Church participated, as well as Jewish and Eastern Orthodox participants for the Old Testament.

New Living Translation, published by Tyndale House Publishers in 1996, is available from many sources, which include Christian bookstores, large 'regular' bookstores, and online resources such as the American Bible Society (www.bibles.com). Bible Gateway (www.biblegateway.com) describes the NLT this way: "The goal of any Bible translation is to convey the meaning of the ancient Greek and Hebrew texts as accurately as possible to the modern reader. The New Living translation is based on the most recent scholarship in the theory of translation. The challenge for the translators was to create a text that would make the same impact in the life of modern readers that the original text had for the original readers. In the New Living Translation, this is accomplished by translating entire thoughts (rather than just words) into natural, everyday English. The end result is a translation that is easy to read and understand and that accurately communicates the meaning of the original text."

The Message, published by NavPress / Eugene Peterson, can be obtained at many Christian bookstores as well as 'regular' large bookstores. The Message can also be ordered through its own website: www.messagebible. com. It is described by the publisher as follows: "Why was *The Message* written? The best answer to that question comes from Eugene Peterson himself: 'While I was teaching a class on Galatians, I began to realize that the adults in my class weren't feeling the vitality and directness that I sensed as I read and studied the New Testament in its original Greek. Writing straight from the original text, I began to attempt to bring into

English the rhythms and idioms of the original language. I knew that the early readers of the New Testament were captured and engaged by these writings and I wanted my congregation to be impacted in the same way. I hoped to bring the New Testament to life for two different types of people: those who hadn't read the Bible because it seemed too distant and irrelevant and those who had read the Bible so much that it had become 'old hat.'

"Peterson's parishioners simply weren't connecting with the real meaning of the words and the relevance of the New Testament for their own lives. So he began to bring into English the rhythms and idioms of the original ancient Greek—writing straight out of the Greek text without looking at other English translations. As he shared his version of Galatians with them, they quit stirring their coffee and started catching Paul's passion and excitement as he wrote to a group of Christians whom he was guiding in the ways of Jesus Christ. For more than two years, Peterson devoted all his efforts to *The Message New Testament*. His primary goal was to capture the tone of the text and the original conversational feel of the Greek, in contemporary English.

"Some people like to read the Bible in Elizabethan English. Others want to read a version that gives a close word-for-word correspondence between the original languages and English. Eugene Peterson recognized that the original sentence structure is very different from that of contemporary English. He decided to strive for the spirit of the original manuscripts—to express the rhythm of the voices, the flavor of the idiomatic expressions, the subtle connotations of meaning that are often lost in English translations.

"The goal of *The Message* is to engage people in the reading process and help them understand what they read. This is not a study Bible, but rather "a reading Bible." The verse numbers, which are not in the original documents, have been left out of the print version to facilitate easy and enjoyable reading. The original books of the Bible were not written in formal language. *The Message* tries to recapture the Word in the words we use today."

Appendix 2

Notes

All stories contained in this book are true. Names and identifying characteristics have been altered, except where persons have given permission to be identified.

Chapter 6

A Passionate Life Workbook, Mike Breen and Walt Kallestad, Cook Communications Ministries, 2005, p. 52.

Chapter 27

A Passionate Life Workbook, Mike Breen and Walt Kallestad, Cook Communications Ministries, 2005, p. 40.

Chapter 32

"Does Anybody Hear Her", Mark Hall, sung by Casting Crowns, recorded on Lifesong CD, Club Zoo Music (BMI), 2005.

About the author

Rev. Dr. Al W. Adams is an ordained pastor in the Christian Church (Disciples of Christ) tradition. She has served in many and varied locations and ministries, which have included hospital and police chaplaincy, congregational leadership, and church planting. Trained in coaching and mediation, she has also served as consultant, mentor, and seminar leader/facilitator for clergy, congregations, and leadership teams. Her passion is bringing individuals and congregations together as Scripture and faith come alive in them, thus enabling them to be and do more than they dare ask...or imagine! (Eph. 3:21) Dr. Al has a BS in Education and a Masters degree in counseling from the University of Missouri, a Masters of Divinity (M.Div.) from Eden Theological Seminary in St. Louis, and a Doctor of Ministry (D.Min.) from Brite Divinity School (Texas Christian University). This is the first book in the 'Exploring...Everyday Stories' series of Bible studies and preaching stories.

The Exploring Series is more than just a great Bible study. Rev. Al has combined her knowledge of the scripture with her gift of telling real life stories to make the scriptures come alive. This series will challenge you to grow in your Everyday journey to intimacy with Christ as you gain deeper understanding of the scriptures. I look forward to each new study and recommend this book to everyone who wants to deepen their walk of faith.

Deb Martin, Deskside Support Specialist, large IT outsourcing company,
Love's Foundation Christian Church, Brighton, CO.

I really enjoy the Exploring series. The series works so well as a Bible study program or as a jump off point for an in-depth discussion. I have used several of these meditations for our staff devotions over the last few years, and they have sparked some great discussions. The stories that pertain to the readings are wonderful, thought provoking, funny, serious, and at times sad. I highly recommend reading and using these nuggets of truth in your life.

Jane Fleischer, St. Luke's Episcopal Church, San Antonio, TX.

I am an old Christian but a new Christian in study of the Bible. Pastor Al has given me new insight into the message the Bible gives to each of us. I LOVE her stories. They speak to my heart, and they provide wonderful images for my mind to mull over. I have a new way to start my prayers with God. As one of the stories says, "Hello Love"- I know God smiles.

Sue Aggson, member, United Methodist Church, Fort Morgan, CO

Made in the USA
Columbia, SC
12 January 2019